The Strong Weak People

For those to whom perfection comes slowly.

Jay Kesler

This book is designed for your personal reading pleasure and profit. It is also designed for group study. A leader's guide with helps and hints for teachers is available from your local Christian bookstore or from the publisher at $1.25.

VICTOR BOOKS

a division of SP Publications, Inc., Wheaton, Illinois
Offices also in Fullerton, California • Whitby, Ontario, Canada • London, England

Third printing, 1977

Unless otherwise noted, Scripture quotations are from the King James Version. Other versions quoted are *The Living Bible* (LB), © by Tyndale House Publishers, Wheaton, Ill., used by permission; the *New American Standard Bible* (NASB), © The Lockman Foundation, 1960, 1962, 1963, 1968, 1971, 1972, 1973; *The New International Version: New Testament* (NIV), © 1973, The New York Bible Society International; and the *New Testament in Modern English* by J. B. Phillips (PH), © 1958, The Macmillan Company.

Library of Congress Card Catalog Number: 76-20918
ISBN: 0-88207-739-2

VICTOR BOOKS
A division of SP Publications, Inc.
P. O. Box 1825 • Wheaton, Ill. 60187

Contents

Introduction

Speaking from painful experience, the Apostle Paul assures us that "in our weakness" Christ shows His strength. This book aims to demonstrate this truth from modern life.

Many Christians would like an antiseptic environment protected from the strains and heartaches of living in a tough world. Even if this were possible, it is doubtful that such a life would be worth living.

It is more realistic to recognize that "the rain falls on the just and the unjust." Adversity is inevitable, and in the struggles of life we can become God-shaped instruments for blessing creation. The process of life is a dynamic experience which the people of God never face alone, as He has promised never to leave us or forsake us. As an added strength we are part of His Church which is equipped to overcome hell.

This book is dedicated to the people whose stories are told in these chapters and whose lives have "helped others in the same trouble." Their honesty, stubbornness, resilience, and faith demonstrate the faithfulness of God in our lives. I have received great strength from their example. I'm sure I would never have been helped by perfect people. It is my prayer that others to whom perfection comes slowly will find this book helpful.

These chapters and the guidebook available in Christian bookstores or from the publisher are presented for individual use and also with small groups and Sunday School classes. As the chapters are discussed and the questions are plumbed for answers, I'm confident we will profit by learning to "bear one another's burdens."

1

A Clue from John

"I'm sorry I can't make the meeting; I promised my son I'd attend his band concert."

The words struck me like a hammer. They came from a man I had admired greatly for some years. He was a key figure in my plans to persuade an influential leader to join our organizational project. Now, with the important meeting all set up, John* was letting me hang because it happened to conflict with his son's school band concert.

All the way to the meeting I grumbled to myself. I even talked to God about it and explained how I'd always put His work first and that dozens, if not hundreds, of times I had bent my personal plans to fit the good of the ministry. As I gobbled my "martyr pills," I thought resentfully of my trusted friend who was putting an appointment with his son ahead of something that had eternal consequences. Hadn't he ever seen one

---

*Names in this book are pseudonyms.

of those Christian plaques that reminded: "With eternity's values in view"? I felt I needed his influence to insure success, and now I'd have to do it alone.

I'd asked my wife and children to "understand my situation" so many times that they didn't plan on my presence anymore. After numerous reminders, they accepted my explanation that "I must get this work done; people are depending on me."

To tell the truth, I had developed an informal definition of Christian dedication that said you can test a man's spiritual loyalty by whether he lets family or personal commitments deflect him from heavenly goals. I'd even put my friends and co-workers into categories according to this definition. The "good guys" were the "can-do" people who would always stretch and give more, and the "bad guys" were the ones who made my priorities ("God's priorities") fit around their own "selfish concerns."

I went to the crucial meeting alone and made an excuse for not being able to "deliver John" to consummate the important arrangements. Inwardly I reflected that the faithful were falling like flies. I drove home not a little upset, filled with a mixture of anger, hurt, and above all, a sense of weary aloneness in carrying the weight of it all.

It was something of the same resentment I'd felt as a small boy when the neighborhood kids came to play with my electric train, erector set, truck, and blocks and then left everything for me to clean up and put back in the boxes. Later I learned to sing with gusto and meaning, "Where duty calls or danger, be never wanting there."

Why is it that some see the work that needs doing and jump in, while others do their own thing and seem to have a clear conscience? I would have liked to keep my promises to my family too. But other people needed me more. I thought John understood spiritual priorities, but here he was letting me down.

I decided to pray. And prayerfully meditate. I loved and respected John too much to be hateful. Overall, he was the kind of man I wanted to be and he had the kind of family I wanted as well. I realized I had missed something somewhere because the whining, martyr spirit within me was not worthy of the Christian faith.

As I prayed, I realized that a band concert is not a small thing to a student participant. How can a son help feeling unimportant if his hard work is always secondary to the "important things Dad has to do"? I realized how often my Janie must have felt put down by my disregard of the details of her daily life. She and our children were preoccupied with "ordinary" things; if these things could always be pushed aside or ignored, a powerful negative message must be sounding toward the person doing these things. It's amazing how prayer clarified my situation!

My definition of eternal values suddenly started to change. What would be valuable a million years from now? Would an earthly organization or institution be around in eternity, or would a wife and son or daughter? It began to become clear that this was what Jesus was trying to impress upon the Pharisees. "The Sabbath was made for man, and not man for the Sabbath" (Mark 2:27). If you have to destroy people to protect the system, what good is the system? I knew that my priorities and value structure had to change and that people had to rank above functions and institutions, even Christian institutions dedicated to serving people.

This began a brand new chapter in my life. Since that day I've watched a lot of men and women, read many books, and talked to hundreds of young people about setting right priorities. Even when carefully formed, they are not always easy to keep and they must have some flexibility, but each person needs to choose his or her own.

Following are some suggestions arising from my struggle. They are not easy to observe faithfully, and sometimes they must give way to each other. But perhaps this can serve as a beginning point for you.

Number One

A Christian's first priority must be a close relationship with God. When we say that we want to follow Christ, it involves a commitment to the quality of life and relationships as described in the Scriptures. Our relationship to God is that of a child to his father, based on love. The consequent value structure does not need a constant policing. As Dr. Milo Rediger of Taylor University has stated, "Love prompts far more than the law demands."

When we love someone, we desire to please that person. We do not feel oppressed by complex rules when living for loved ones. There are laws in society, for instance, against beating my wife or starving my children. In all of the years of our marriage, however, the police have never come to our house to enforce those laws. We love one another, and love lives above the minimal requirements.

When Jesus was asked about the complex system of Jewish law, He answered, "Thou shalt love the Lord thy God with all thy heart, and with all thy soul, and with all thy mind. This is the first and great commandment" (Matt. 22:37-38).

Loving God must be distinguished from fulfilling religious exercises. Many rigorously fill their lives with religious meetings and duties, equating these with keeping the great commandment of Jesus. But to love God is to love what He loves, and He loves people supremely.

In Germany's Reformation days, the churches were besieged by iconoclasts. Revolting against the formalism of out-ward religion, the dissidents smashed the symbols and statuary that had become objects of worship. Though the stone icons were banished, invisible idols were not so readily eliminated. They persist in many forms, sometimes as hyperactive religious activity and the building of religious empires.

We should understand that God's priorities do not line up like the pictures in biology books showing a small fish being eaten by a larger fish which is in turn eaten by a larger fish which vanishes inside a still larger one. We do not accomplish God's goal by destroying someone to reach it. God's concerns are comprehensive and include all of His children's concerns. He is put first by putting His children and their welfare first. A man who neglects his family for church work may reap the same harvest of alienation as one who neglects his family for the country club. God cannot be worshiped in a vacuum; He is worshiped in word and deed that touch humanity as well as heaven.

Number Two

Second is a commitment to ourselves—which is not as strange as it may sound. After giving the first commandment, Jesus continued, "And the second is like unto it, Thou shalt love thy neighbor as thyself" (Matt. 22:39). If one does not love himself, his neighbor is in for trouble! Many, if not most, hos-tilities toward others begin in ourselves. An unforgiven man is unforgiving toward others; an unloved man is unloving.

Some Christians seem to believe that verses such as Gala-tians 2:20, "I am crucified with Christ," require some sort of personality kamikaze—that they must constantly put down and trample themselves to please God. This verse does not speak of the ego but of egotism, that self-centered spirit that makes us want to have our way at the expense of our neighbor. To feel concerned for myself is not pride in the negative sense. There are two kinds of pride. One is the opposite of humility; that's bad. The other is the opposite of shame; that's good! Taking care of our bodies and our minds is service to God. Proper diet, exercise, and rest honor God, whose temple we are (1 Cor. 3:16-17).

It has become a badge of distinction in some circles to say, "I haven't taken a vacation in five years." It is hard to conceive of a person bragging, "I overeat and get drunk constantly." Yet there is a similarity in the two statements. Both are indications of intemperance and both are harmful to the individual. It is difficult for "workaholics" to explain why Jesus retreated from the press of people by getting in a boat and going across the Sea of Galilee. That God saw fit to "rest" on the seventh day should mean something to us mere humans about respite from labor and demands upon our energies.

Discussions of priorities are superfluous if we are dead or crippled by neglect of our legitimate needs. For many years I was driven by a slogan of a zealous missionary: "Burn out; don't rust out." Now I'm convinced that this does not state the alternatives properly.

Number Three

The third priority, according to Jesus, is the neighbor category, and I have divided it into four groups.

1. *Husband/Wife*   If one is married, his or her spouse ranks ahead of other "neighbors." I would separate the husband or wife from the children because, if the marriage relationship is not intact, the children suffer no matter how much "quality time" and effort goes in.

Verbal assurances are needed for each spouse to sense his importance to the other. Gestures and symbols are also important indicators of where we are in our mate's priority list. A phone call to check on a wife's well-being or to question her about her day will speak volumes, as will flowers, perfume, or a card. On the flip side, so will a batch of favorite cookies, an unsolicited hug or smile or other private communication such as a note in a lunch bucket or a pocket.

2. *Children*   Is there any area of greater anxiety than our children? Unfortunately, parents are usually struggling to find their own identity, learning to know each other as marriage partners, and establishing themselves economically when their young children need extra attention. About the time children become teens, most parents discover they are strangers in the same house. Often a feverish attempt follows to spend time together, but the young adults (not children) prefer independence and privacy.

Many helpful things have been written on this and other crises in rearing children, but if a child understands that his parents love God, are committed to each other, and together see him as special, he will sense a basic security that gives resilience to cope with parental inadequacies.

Some young people try increasingly bizzare behavior until an action, however destructive, gets their parents' attention. I've heard boys say, "He couldn't find a day for me, but the judge made him find one to appear with me in court."

Scripture does not say, "He that doth not work" or "He that does not win souls" is worse than an infidel, but "He that [careth] not for his own . . ." (1 Tim. 5:8). Proper priorities rather than good intentions can head off most of these problems. Family nights together, promises kept, meals together, remembering birthdays—these are strong links in family life.

It is amazing how we can find time for each other in a crisis. An "indispensable man" who must work day and night, cannot miss any meeting, and must check everything personally, can catch the flu or have a coronary—and somehow life goes on without him.

Perhaps this is the greatest fear! Parents who have seen their children rebel with drugs, sex, or delinquent behavior have discovered that family priorities are like maintenance on a car or building. You either practice them or a major breakdown will force drastic response eventually. It is the natural consequence of neglect. Those ounces of prevention avoid the necessity of severe cures.

3. *Friends*   Every Christian needs a group of caring people with whom he spends enough time and honesty to have "covenant relationships." By this I mean committing ourselves to one another as brothers and sisters in Christ so that we will "drop everything" to support one another in time of need. To know that there are people committed to us in this way is a strength beyond words, a cord of many strands. Many Christians want such relationships but are not yet willing to spend the time and effort to deepen friendships. Remember that the disciples were not constantly serving others and performing miracles. They walked and talked together, probed personalities, cooked, and ate, etc. On these foundations God built their friendship and commitment to each other.

Scripture teaches us that fellowship is not a means but an end (1 John 1:1-4). Too often we see people as instruments to get something done and feel guilty unless we have a discussion agenda or significant reason for getting together. Some Christians need to learn to "waste time together," to dignify each other by acknowledging: "You are important enough that I just want to be with you, not to get you to do something or share something." No one wants to be a function or to be used. People need people because God made us that way, and meeting this need must be built into our priorities.

4. *Society at large*   We touch this group of neighbors in

many ways—in our neighborhoods, through our work, as citizens in a society.

Some would say, "How can I make a living if all this comes before my work?" But to get our priorities straight we need to ask ourselves, "What kind of life do I give to my work?" A man or woman who is committed to God, acting in healthy self-esteem, enjoying a happy marriage and secure children, and is being affirmed by friends brings a valued and effective contribution to any employment.

Proper priorities do not just happen. The Enemy of souls works constantly to worm into the warp and woof of our life fabric. Full commitment to God through Christ is the first step toward spiritual success. This commitment is not simply singing "I Surrender All." It involves measuring all my activities against the principles of the Word of God and the example of Jesus Christ. We are never left alone to work our way through disappointment, but the basic principles of Scripture and the power of the Holy Spirit produce progress and harmony in our lives. God made us and He can maintain us!

Study Questions
Read 1 Peter 5:7; Matthew 22:37-39; 1 John 1:1-4; 1 Timothy 5:8; Ephesians 5:22-23, 25.
1. Name some modern obstacles to these priorities.
2. What can a person do if there are more things to do than time or energy allows after setting priorities?
3. When do you feel more like a function than a person?
4. How may the weight of our responsibilities be shared in a biblical way?
5. Does anyone in the group share a "covenant relationship" he or she is willing to describe?

2

The Family That Failed Together

It was a hot Sunday evening in August. I had just finished speaking at the evening service in a prestigious Eastern suburban church. As I stood in the foyer, I noticed a man beside me waiting for the others to leave. I sensed he wanted to speak to me alone.

"I know you are busy," he said, "but I'm confused and need some help." He introduced himself as Bob.

"Why don't we sit down," I said as I took off my jacket and loosened my tie.

"My wife, Marj, and I have been members of this church for almost 30 years," he began. "We've been faithful to the services, held many church offices, and participated in neighborhood visitation programs. We've really wanted to be used by the Lord, but somehow all of our activities seem to stay on the surface. You would think our church work would have gotten us into the 'in' group but it didn't. We had just assumed that all the people with problems were outside the church and those of us in the church had the answers to all of our problems."

My knitted eyebrows may have slowed him momentarily, then he went on.

"I suppose most churches are made up of people like us. People who work hard in a variety of programs but never seem to be of specific spiritual help to anyone. However, last year all this changed."

"What happened?" I asked, searching for a key to his obvious bewilderment.

"Well, it's rather embarrassing," he said, "but since everyone in our community knows about it, I'll tell you. We believed Ken, the youngest of our three children, to be about as normal as a boy could be. Oh, we've had a few problems, but who hasn't? He got good grades in school. We're not rich, but we were able to provide most everything a boy could want. He had a job and we thought he was headed for college. To make a long story short, I visited him this afternoon in the state penitentiary."

Then, answering my question before I asked, he explained, "I guess you've got to have the whole story or it doesn't make sense. Our boy was involved with some others in a series of crimes which resulted in an armed robbery. Ken was arrested and the story was in all the papers and on television. Before the trial was over, everyone knew about it.

"There was no place to hide. My wife and I were ashamed to go out of the house for several days. Over and over we asked God how this could be. Why us? How could we face people?

"We finally decided to go to the grocery store together, and though nothing happened, we felt ostracized from society —all alone in the world. Everyone seemed to be staring at us. On Sunday we went to church, and our shame and fear made us stick together like burrs. Now here's my point."

We both knew the story so far was only a prologue to the

real issue. Bob's shame and struggle seemed to have been replaced by a new problem.

"Like I said, as far as I can tell I've never been of spiritual help to anyone. But since our trouble and all the publicity, we've had a constant stream of people from the church coming to us for spiritual help. Why is it that when you're doing well the relationships in church are smooth and formal, and people hardly noticing you, and now that we have all these troubles with our family everyone is telling us theirs as if we know some secret?"

Bob's frustration showed in his flushed face and outstretched hands. When he regained his composure, he continued.

"Here's the way I've got it figured out, and I want you to tell me if I'm on the right track. It seems to me that when people take a super-spiritual pose in church, pretending they have no problems, all the other church people are afraid to be honest with them for fear that they will look like failures because they have problems. It's really strange that when we were trying our best and, on the surface at least, succeeding in our Christian lives, we didn't touch any other lives. Now that we have had so many problems with our own child, everyone wants our help—everyone wants to know how the Lord is working out our problem. We never dreamed so many people in our congregation were hurting with personal and family problems. What do you think?"

As Bob talked I thought of my own reactions in time of personal failure. As a boy in high school I remembered what happened when exam grades were passed out. The students with A's mingled casually and the kids with D's and F's never came near. If you had a low grade, it was tough to find an understanding friend until someone with the same or worse problem turned up. I agreed with my new friend that we were learning how people are able to help each other.

Adding a postscript to the conversation, the thoughtful father said, "This afternoon my son put his hand on my shoulder and said, 'Dad, I know I've caused you and Mom a lot of trouble and pain. I want you to know I'm sorry and I love you both more than I can tell you.' You know, I'd go through everything, including the shame, except for the man shot in the robbery, just to have him say that to me and feel his hand on my shoulder. My wife and I have learned so much through all of this about ourselves, our brothers and sisters in Christ, and about our relationship with our kids. I'm not saying it's good to do bad things, but it's been a truly good experience."

The Right to Be Weak

This account had a profound effect on me and prompted me to reexamine my own relationships. I began to wonder who started the lie that Christians have to succeed all the time. Perhaps some of it stems from always putting people who have succeeded up in front of congregations and youth groups. This technique may be good strategy for sales motivation meetings but it seems to have done great harm to the church. In a world where success models are spotlighted and failures are shunted into the shadows we have learned to mask our feelings and defeats.

Paul speaks clearly of the help we should be to one another. "Blessed be God, even the Father of our Lord Jesus Christ, the Father of mercies, and the God of all comfort; who comforteth us in all our tribulation, that we may be able to comfort them which are in any trouble, by the comfort wherewith we ourselves are comforted of God. For as the sufferings of Christ abound in us, so our consolation also aboundeth by Christ" (2 Cor. 1:3-5).

As we are willing to open ourselves to one another, we discover the strength of bearing each other's burdens. If we allow others to see the help we have found in Christ in time of crisis, they can be strengthened and encouraged by "someone who has been there."

Deep interpersonal relationships must begin on the surface and work their way in. Discussions of "safe" subjects are not a waste of time and should be the beginning point. It's tragic, however, when various members of the body of Christ are unable after many years to express their feelings to each other and seek help.

Paul linked his weakness to God's strength: "My grace is sufficient for thee; for My strength is made perfect in weakness. . . . For when I am weak [said Paul] then am I strong" (2 Cor. 12:9-10).

Paul led from his weakness. Most of us know this principle but don't practice it. Often it takes a tragedy or an open failure to bring this reality into our lives.

In Bob's family's case, newspaper publicity, television, and radio spoke their shame into every home. Unknown to them, however, were the fears and failures of many acquaintances, including fellow church members who needed help. When a family surfaced with real problems, other sufferers suddenly became visible.

An Atmosphere of Helping Others
How can churches develop an atmosphere which would help us to "bear one another's burdens"?

First of all, we can't bear one another's burdens if we aren't willing to admit we have any. It takes a healthy self-esteem and confidence in the grace of God to remove the mask that some of us have learned to wear. Our competent, masked self has been accepted by our group of friends and we fear that if they see our real selves and discover our weaknesses they will no longer like us. A great transformation will begin to take place in any congregation when Christians begin to love one another enough that they can be truthful. Masked lives produce masked responses and superficial relationships. Open, honest lives produce friendliness and compassion.

One of the favorite tricks of Satan is to cause us to feel that our problems and failings are different from anyone else's. There is a spiritual as well as political truth in the slogan, "United we stand, divided we fall."

A second advance is made when we realize the falseness of the abbreviated Bible verse: "All things work together for good." This phrase wrenched from Romans 8:28 is quoted by many Christians as being a biblical truth, but this incomplete form is not only untrue to reality, it is dangerous to those who follow it. The whole verse adds: "to them that love God, to them who are the called according to His purpose."

The experiences of life can be cruel, evil, and confusing. It is only as we turn *toward* God rather than *away* from Him during these experiences that they become "good." Guilt, loneliness, isolation, self-contempt, and suicide are some results of turning away from God. But forgiveness, grace, understanding, healing, and fortitude are good results of turning toward Him.

For every couple strengthened through their trial, there are others who are crippled by similar circumstances. They are driven by guilt and shock to shamed withdrawal. They punish themselves and each other for their shortcomings and lapses, and, instead of turning the circumstance into good, evil is compounded. This verse is "reactive" in the sense that our response in time of evil and adversity must allow the process of God's redemption to come full circle. Sometimes lessons cannot be learned nor traits refined except in creative suffering. As we turn toward God in adversity, all circumstances do work together for good.

This good is the result of "loving God." Love in this sense is not something you *feel,* but something you *do.* Job's comforters had to learn this by watching the great object lesson of his life. "Curse God and die" would not produce good, but "Though He slay me, yet will I trust Him" did! (Job 13:15)

In the midst of great difficulty people realize their need for help. In the case of my friend's experience, not only did the tragedy and sense of failure bring him and his wife closer together, but possibly it restored their son as they clung to God. It also transformed the quality of their church life.

Words alone can lose much of their effectiveness in winning people to Jesus Christ. Demonstrations of Christian reality manifested in relationships within the church are a strong affirmation of the Gospel message. As we read the epistles, we see the emphasis on applied Christianity—the living Christ at work in our lives is the message people need to see in the world today.

Christ speaks to us in the midst of our failure, pain, and sorrow as well as in our triumphs. More people in the world are hurting than are successful and happy. For this reason, the Incarnation of Jesus has spoken to people of all strata in all eras. As He was "a man of sorrows, and acquainted with grief" (Isa. 53:3), our own identification with suffering mankind gives us a believable ministry to the world.

Study Questions

Read Romans 8:28; 2 Corinthians 12:9-10; 2 Corinthians 1:3-4.

1. What strengths prepared Bob and his family for their ordeal?
2. What situations do you know personally that have caused

people to turn away from God and the church in time of difficulty?

3. Has your congregation been "conditioned" to mask feelings and cover personal weaknesses because of pride? If so, how?

4. When publicity does not force situations into the open, in what ways may Christians intervene to give help?

5. In churches where members' failings and needs are readily known, what spiritual problems are likely to be prominent?

6. What guidelines are needed for Christians who have decided to be more open to each other?

3

To Witness or Not to Witness

I was impressed with Chuck's candor when he first told me point-blank he'd been fired. Most people soften the embarrassment with statements such as, "I've been let go," "They've done away with my job," "They've passed me by for a younger man," "They're cutting back," or "The new boss is bringing his own crew." Those statements may be accurate, or they may be a cover-up, but Chuck wasn't hiding anything; his boss didn't want him.

I was about to encourage Chuck and make a few phone calls in search of new work when he said, "I've been penalized for my faith. My boss just won't tolerate a clear witness for Christ. He said if I didn't stop telling people about my religion he'd have to let me go. So I put the Lord to the test and now I've been fired."

Wisely Sharing the Faith
As Chuck's story unfolded, I began to have second thoughts. I discovered he had been putting Gospel tracts in the lockers

of his fellow workers. In addition he had posted church meeting announcements on the plant bulletin board and been involved in prolonged doctrinal arguments. This had alienated him from most of the men in the plant, but his aggressive personality didn't allow this to deter him. He continued to start each conversation with a statement about his faith which almost always ended with the other man walking away or someone running interference so the man could get back to work. When Chuck became aware he was the brunt of the plant's crude humor, he shrugged it off with, "I guess this is what being persecuted for Christ means."

Many Christians would say Chuck just didn't use his head. Others, while perhaps feeling uneasy over their own lack of on-the-job witnessing, might criticize Chuck for stealing his employer's time. Some might fault him for zeal without wisdom. If Chuck was insensitive to his fellow workers, how can Christians wisely share their faith with co-workers?

First we should define what we mean by witness. Many Christians view witnessing as verbal only—talking for God. Those who hold this viewpoint forget that a biblical concept of witness is more than something a Christian *does;* it's what he *is.*

The non-Christian knows talk is cheap. Like you and me, he is interested more in performance and attitude than words. He wants to see how the Christian "walks his talk." Witness involves talking, attitude, response under stress, sharing experiences and much more. It's an event, a process, and a way of life. One can witness in a shared elevator, at a toll booth, in an airplane, on the job, or in the home. The style and content vary with different situations.

One can hardly conceive of a more complicated mission than when God began to communicate Himself to us. We notice that He did not communicate everything at once, nor did He always use the same method. Chuck needed someone to help him see there is more to witnessing than preaching. Being God's "peculiar" people (1 Peter 2:9) does not mean to be odd because we lack politeness or sensitivity. And it doesn't mean we should witness out of a sense of guilt or duty.

Three Levels of Communication

With Peter's encouragement to follow in Christ's steps (1 Peter 2:21), let's look at three levels of communication in our Saviour's methods.

1. *Biblical Truth* The first level involves unequivocal statements of biblical truth. The Christian has the responsibility to verbally declare these truths from Scripture.

"All have sinned and come short of the glory of God" (Rom. 3:23); "The soul that sinneth, it shall die" (Ezek. 18:4); and "For the wages of sin is death; but the gift of God is eternal life through Jesus Christ our Lord" (Rom. 6:23) are examples of essential biblical truth. Yet the effective Christian must be sensitive to the tone of his voice and the manner in which he presents these truths. The wise Christian knows he must not use Scripture as a club to bludgeon people into the kingdom of God.

Some people are combative by nature and feel they are making no impression unless the person to whom they are witnessing becomes angry. Such people are like a man I know who didn't feel his pastor had preached the Gospel when he left church not feeling guilty. People subjected to guilt-pressure techniques often react like an overheated boiler. The inner tension produces a tight-lipped, humorless life which is attractive to no one. The joy and love streaming from reconciliation with God are the true, appealing qualities of the "Good News."

Jesus often wrapped truths in stories to gain attention and penetration when straight facts might offend His hearers. Always the perfect teacher, Jesus drew people out and encouraged them to correlate realities they already knew. He then communicated eternal truth and shared the reality of Himself.

Proper timing, a sense of the appropriate comment, and knowledge of a person's background are factors to consider when witnessing with words. I recall being frustrated in an unsuccessful attempt to convince a young man of the necessity of trusting Christ. In my eagerness to win him, I did not bother to understand the reason for his resistance. A few months earlier his mother had committed suicide, and somehow he believed if he received Christ for his own salvation he would condemn his mother's soul because of her unbelief. What a noble emotion! How terrible of me to violate such feelings. My timing was wrong; his understanding was deficient. It was no time for sermons. It was time for patience, love, and healing.

2. *Relational Truth* Sometimes words are not the most effective method for witnessing. A second way to communicate God's redeeming love is through relational truth. This involves developing friendship and rapport with an individual and demonstrating the validity of the Gospel by living experiences. "Christ became [a man] and dwelt among us" (see John 1:14); "Jesus wept" (John 11:35); "He was despised and rejected of men; a man of sorrows, and acquainted with grief" (Isa. 53:3). Jesus communicated God's ways and requirements by His deeds as well as His words.

I met a young man in South Africa who wanted to win a friend to Christ, but the friend wouldn't listen. He was a marathon runner who slogged 26 miles every Saturday morning. The Christian began to run with his friend and found that as their friendship grew he stopped thinking of his companion as a target of evangelism. As his attitude changed, his friend inquired about his concerns and goals and the door to words was opened. The witness of life had unlocked the entrance.

We can extol the virtues of truthfulness, but the day-to-day experience of dealing with a truthful man will speak more forcefully. A father can preach to a son about experiencing the forgiveness of Christ, but a son forgiven by a father receives a clear communication. Conversely, a father who asks forgiveness demonstrates an equally useful truth.

Words take on the character of the speaker. They are automatically put in context by listeners. The witness for Christ must be validated by actions, sometimes over a period of time.

A young man once asked, "Will you still be my friend if I don't accept your Jesus?" He was testing whether he was a part of a project or a person to be loved. Christ confirmed the genuineness of His words to the moment of His death when He said, "Father, forgive them; for they know not what they do" (Luke 23:34). Jesus demonstrated that He was no fair-weather friend.

3. *Truth Fleshed Out*   The third level of God's communication to us is incarnational, that is, God in flesh. Jesus not only revealed God by words and actions, He was God Himself. Jesus embodied the very nature of God. The writer of 1 Corinthians 6:19 tells us that God the Holy Spirit lives in believers' bodies, and Galatians 5:22-23 describes the potential results: "But when the Holy Spirit controls our lives He will produce this kind of fruit in us: love, joy, peace, patience, kindness, goodness, faithfulness, gentleness, and self-control; and here there is no conflict with Jewish laws" (LB). And I might add there is no conflict with modern laws either!

To embody these virtues of Christ by the power of the Holy Spirit is to be conformed to the image of God's Son (see Rom. 8:29). Many people will never read a Bible seriously or listen to a witness until they have seen God's love in a human being. One of the most eloquent passages in all literature begins, "Though I speak with the tongues of men and of angels, and have not love, I am become as sounding brass, or a tinkling cymbal" (1 Cor. 13:1). Sentimental and shallow expressions of "love" are not convincing, but when godly love produces the actions and attitudes described in 1 Corinthians 13, a powerful witness to God is displayed.

Imagine someone working in a plant or office or living next door who could be described as follows: "He suffers long, and is kind; he envies not; he vaunts not himself, is not puffed up. He does not behave unseemly, seeks not his own only, is not easily provoked, thinks no evil, rejoices not in iniquity, but rejoices in the truth; bears all things, believes all things, hopes through all things, endures all things" (see 1 Cor. 13:4-7). To back up a verbal witness with these virtues would amplify the Gospel beyond the power of the most sophisticated media!

A Christian is obviously more limited in communication skills than Jesus. It follows then that our witness, like His, must involve more than words. Chuck paid the price of easy words, not of high-cost love. His troubles stemmed from a gross misunderstanding of the Great Commission and the nature of effective communication. Chuck himself, not the Lord, was on display, and Chuck failed the test badly.

If we show love as well as speak it and are still rejected, we must remember that neither Jesus nor His apostles were always accepted. Despite their godly power, they suffered and most of them became martyrs.

Jesus warned us that we could expect the same treatment, but He assured us He will never leave us or forsake us. Our suffering is shared by Him.

Still, God has promised to bring life from some of the

Gospel seed we plant and water. If we lose our source of livelihood through witnessing, God will provide another. But let's be sure the "offense of the Cross," not our own obnoxiousness, generates the opposition. It is good to remember that God is at work quietly even when we are not present. He loves people more than we do, and He has supernatural power at His disposal. The joy of witness results from making ourselves available to the sovereign direction of the Holy Spirit.

Study Questions

Read Philippians 2:5-16; 2 Corinthians 5:17-21; John 17:16-26; John 15:1-27; 1 Timothy 4:12; Ephesians 6:5-8.
1. What discrepancy, if any, exists between what you believe (or what you've been told) about witnessing and your performance?
2. Give examples of witnessing that you admire. What are their first-, second-, and third-level characteristics?
3. Is rejection and suffering for Christ experienced today? If so, give examples.
4. When are rejection and suffering self-induced? Give illustrations.
5. What do you believe should be the primary motivation for witness?
6. Discuss the main point of 1 Timothy 4:12. What is meant by "conversation" in the King James Version?

4

Confessions of a Traveling Man

I was sitting with a roomful of businessmen at a men's retreat when one man ventured: "I wonder what the Apostle Paul would do if he had my job. In fact, I wonder if he could make it at all." Understanding laughter greeted the remark, followed by knowing glances from man to man. I was the only "man of the cloth" present, and I was in the dark. Since my ministry is with laymen, I decided not to let the opportunity pass without using it to get a deeper insight into their lives.

"You men know me," I said, "and know I empathize with your struggles. What is it about your jobs you think I wouldn't understand?"

Phil, the man who triggered it all, responded. "Okay," he said, "here's the situation I face. I'm a traveling factory representative and I get lonely when I'm away from home. If I'm traveling with other men or meeting for a conference at some hotel, I naturally want to be included in the group. When the working day is finished, most want to go to the bar for a drink, and I feel uncomfortable in that kind of place. If I go to my room, I stare at the walls."

Phil shifted uneasily, then decided to take some risks.

"Television is zero, I've read all the magazines, so what can I do? Sometimes I go to movies, but that's getting more and more useless. Either they're some kid thing or they're grossly 'adult.' I've gone to some of the adult movies and felt degraded afterwards.

"That's only the beginning. Sometimes I face sexual temptations. Other guys pick up women or have women come to their rooms—you can't believe how some 'decent' people behave away from home!"

I glanced around for reactions of the other men and concluded this was what the knowing glances were about.

"Now don't get me wrong," Phil added. "I've never given in to these temptations, but sometimes I get anxious about my thought patterns. If it's true that 'as a man thinks in his heart, so is he,' then I have a problem."

I was reminded of John Wesley's comment that you can't keep birds, like temptations, from flying over your head, but you can keep them from nesting in your hair.

Phil's words reminded me of Romans 7 being played on a tape recorder in a recent paraphrase:

"I don't understand myself at all, for I really want to do what is right, but I can't. I do what I don't want to—what I hate. I know perfectly well that what I am doing is wrong, and my bad conscience proves that I agree with these laws I am breaking. But I can't help myself, because I'm no longer doing it. It is sin inside me that is stronger than I am that makes me do these evil things.

"I know I am rotten through and through so far as my old sinful nature is concerned. No matter which way I turn I can't make myself do right. I want to but I can't. When I want to do good, I don't; and when I try not to do wrong, I do it anyway. Now if I am doing what I don't want to, it is plain where the trouble is: sin still has me in its evil grasp.

"It seems to be a fact of life that when I want to do what is right, I inevitably do what is wrong. I love to do God's will so far as my new nature is concerned, but there is something else deep within me, in my lower nature, that is at war with my mind and wins the fight and makes me a slave to the sin that is still within me. In my mind I want to be God's willing servant but instead I find myself still enslaved to sin.

"So you see how it is: my new life tells me to do right, but the old nature that is still inside me loves to sin. Oh, what a terrible predicament I'm in! Who will free me from my slavery to this deadly lower nature? Thank God! It has been done by Jesus Christ our Lord. He has set me free" (Rom. 7:15-25, LB).

I thought Phil was through, but he continued. "If this is not enough," he said, "I'm under pressure from the other regional managers. They turn in expense accounts that pretty well match each other's—except for mine that runs one-half to two-thirds as high as theirs. They feel my life-style is OK for me, but when it makes them look bad to the boss, they don't appreciate me."

It is amazing how pressures to conform reach into all areas of life. I can remember my difficulty in explaining to my son how tattling on others would make him disliked. I have a lasting impression of the West Point cadet who observed the honor code by exposing himself and others for cribbing on exams and reaped hate from fellow cadets as well as officers. Let's face it—we're not supposed to rock the boat!

One of the other men suggested: "Why not share the situation in general terms with your boss?"

"I've thought of that," said Phil, "but I feel sure he's doing much the same in other ways and I'm the one who's out of step. The only way out for me may be to get another job."

Other men began to share their frustrations, and it became evident that the grass was not necessarily greener across the fences for others either!

With details changed here and there, the stories I've heard repeat Phil's narrative. Many Christians seem to believe that it's not possible to live their beliefs in their work environment. Some Christians who feel they can maintain personal purity and marital fidelity worry about being corrupted by questionable business practices. They see payoffs, kickbacks, wining and dining customers, favors and deals becoming standard business practice.

The lessons of Watergate will be spelled out to us for years to come. It is a source of wonderment to me that some people in church circles justify guilty participants by pointing out that both political parties have been doing similar things for years. I wonder how these people would deal with children who defend themselves with the claim that "all the kids are doing it."

Two wrongs do not make a right. A dynamic tension must always exist between the Christian and the world: two standards are in conflict, yet they must continue to interact. To throw up our hands in resignation is betrayal of Christ. The struggle itself has value to both ourselves and our world.

Because no Bible personality ever worked for a multinational company, rode a jet, saw a computer printout, or had an expense account, some Christians think the Bible has no help for our modern predicaments. True, there are no exact biblical counterparts to modern situations, but basic honesty and godly responsibility are the same in every time frame. We find helpful biblical insights into the nature of the very things Phil talked about.

Satan's Trickery

One of Satan's favorite tricks is to isolate us emotionally. He wants us to think our temptations are unique and we're the only ones with such problems. The devil is described in the Bible as a roaring lion seeking whom he may devour (1 Peter 5:8). Wily lions attack the sheep at the edge of the flock, the one ranging farthest from the shepherd. The Apostle Paul said, "There hath no temptation taken you but such as is common to man; but God is faithful, who will not suffer you to be tempted above that ye are able; but will with the temptation also make a way to escape, that ye may be able to bear it" (1 Cor. 10:13).

We find several helpful insights in this paragraph. First, temptation is common to all people. And James said, "Blessed is the man who endureth temptation, for when he is tried he shall receive the crown of life" (1:12). If you have not known temptation, you cannot overcome it, and only overcomers receive crowns. We are not tempted by some incomprehensible fog seeping under our door, but by recognizable compromises or bold assaults against our minds, emotions, and bodies. Since Satan cannot create, he corrupts good things God made for our well-being and enjoyment.

For every temptation there is a moral, God-ordained outlet. This is what Paul was talking about when he said that with the temptation there is a way to escape. We get further insights into this truth in Philippians: "Whatsoever things are true, whatsoever things are honest, whatsoever things are just, whatsoever things are pure, whatsoever things are lovely, whatsoever things are of good report; if there be any virtue, and if there be any praise, think on these things" (4:8). Not only does God counsel us how to flee evil, but He provides a positive preventative. Thinking about pure and constructive things avoids contamination and capture by evil.

It is dangerous to focus on the temptation. This heightens the tension and fascination. Many lonely men reinforce their temptations by dwelling on them introspectively until God's perspective is submerged.

Suppose I told you to stop reading and think of anything you wish except a huge, pink elephant whose head touches one wall of your room, whose tail touches the other wall and whose back reaches to the ceiling. Think of anything *except* this elephant! The allurement of the forbidden is strong unless you occupy your mind and body with what God approves.

Practical Strategy

Some practical helps involve initiating activities which will hold your interest and sustain you during free hours. Phone calls home should be considered as important and legitimate by the absent father as the family's food and clothing. Following the family's progress by phone and checking in with each child can remind you of your family responsibility.

It is helpful to be reminded that we fulfill many roles: spouse, parent, citizen, church member, and neighbor as well as breadwinner. We can receive support from many sources. With a little advanced planning, you can attend church functions and develop wholesome friendships in other cities while away from home. A bit of investigation can usually discover a concert or sporting event to attend.

Routine is also helpful. A man on the road can go to his room, take a short nap, shower, shave, put on a clean shirt, and eat a leisurely dinner. Later, to prepare for bed and sleep, light work or reading wraps up a day. I've been able to maintain a rewarding reading schedule by carrying books on several subjects and of varying complexity on trips. If I'm not in the mood to handle heavy reading, a good novel is often just what I need. Some men study correspondence courses in their extra time. Systematic, serious Bible study should not be beyond any layperson. Sometimes a workout at a local gym or steam room is a good way to end the day.

Specific prayer for each member of your family before you go to sleep will minimize the fantasy problem and assist pleasant dreams. A traveling man or a man at home needs to begin each day with the Lord and end it with his hand in the Lord's. Don't let circumstances or the devil make your appointments; plan them with the Lord. Take charge!

Corporate Compromises

Corporate sins and compromises are another ball game. The proverb "Virtue is its own reward" has been laughed out of fashion. Its successor whispers persuasively: "Do unto others before they do unto you."

All honest men do not get promoted. The hardest workers often do not get paid more. Honesty is sometimes the losing policy. But these are true only in the short run and on human scales. The prosperity of chiselers is not a modern problem. David spent a good deal of time lamenting the apparent success of evil men.

There is still evidence that honest representation of the product, fair pricing, and consistent delivery builds consumer confidence and financial success. But there is national and international evidence that strict honesty entails a penalty that many find undesirable and unnecessary. Some are convinced that bribes are unavoidable and therefore right. Such ignorance of God's standard and concern spells long-range doom. Christians must never forget that God will ultimately— if not immediately—judge these corrupt practices.

Abraham Lincoln called the nation to believe that "right makes might"—a powerful truth for nation and individual alike.

The story of Joseph in Genesis 39—41 contains a principle with a long-term promise. Joseph's commitment to honesty and fair dealing caused him to rise above every circumstance. Yet, the environment of evil caused him constant difficulty and heartache.

The warnings of Jesus to His disciples in John 15 and 16 are aimed at preparing Christians for the disappointment and pain of following Him in this world. Many have attempted to escape these difficult experiences by quitting their jobs, but God's men in Scripture stayed by their responsibilities and became witnesses to His truth amongst opposition. After the shepherds saw and heard the angels and beheld the Saviour, they returned to their flocks. Changed shepherds, not full-time priests, was the result. This is one of the implications of the Reformers' stress on the priesthood of every believer. It not only means that we have personal access to God through Christ, but that we are ministering priests in every area and occupation of life.

Maintaining a Christian stance in the midst of these pressures is no easy task. Yet there is an identifiable thread throughout Jesus' teachings that in sharing His sufferings we testify of Him and His truth. We are also assured that sufferers will share in His glory (Phil. 1:27—2:18; 2 Tim. 2:12). Patient enduring of the pains and rejections of life testifies of God's rewards already in this life (1 Peter 2:19-25).

We are to be not only the "light of the world" and "salt of the earth," but also "sheep among wolves" (Matt. 5:13-14; 10:16). As citizens of Christ's kingdom we serve a different master from the world's. We march to a different drumbeat. The Christian remembers that his holy God will have the final word on human affairs and that at "His name every knee shall bow and every tongue shall confess Jesus Christ is Lord" (see Phil. 2:10-11).

Study Questions
   Read 1 Corinthians 10:12-14; James 4:1-10; Philippians
1:27—2:18; 4:6-9; 1 Peter 2:19-25.
1. How strong is the relationship between our physical, emo-
   tional, and spiritual natures? Are we more vulnerable to
   sin in times of failure and depression?
2. Suggest additional positive activities that would counteract
   temptations.
3. Is there a need among Christians for a different kind of
   measurement of success than ones in current use? Some
   possibilities?
4. Describe examples of honesty, sobriety, and fidelity that
   have helped achieve success.
5. What compromises do you face in your occupation?
6. What tactics have helped you handle occupational conflicts
   in ethics?
7. If you fail in a moral situation, would you be able to share
   the hurt with a church member? Why or why not?

5

Winning the Rat Race

Every once in a while I meet a person who is hurting and I'm frustrated because I can't do much more than agree that it's a tough world.

One night Alan, a building contractor of custom-built homes, came to me with his chin on his chest. "Man, I've had it," he said. "They got me coming and going. I can't win." I encouraged him to explain and he told me his story.

"First off," he said, "there's the problem of bidding. With the inflationary prices on materials changing without notice, it's almost impossible for me to come in with a good bid. My competition seems to have no problem with promising one thing and delivering another. I try my best not to do this, but if you don't fudge a little, sometimes you'd lose your shirt. People don't care if you go broke. All they want to do is beat down your price, then show no mercy if you run into difficulty."

I could sense it had been "one of those days" for Alan.

"It's getting so you can't make a promise and keep it," he

continued. "I guess everyone in our business misses deadlines, but I try not to. It's my intention to always give plenty of lead time and not give promises I can't keep, but customers always try and push you into a corner for a completion date. Can I help it if a plumber doesn't come when he promised or they deliver the wrong sink? I sometimes feel if I never saw another person it would be too soon!"

I could see that Alan was hurt, the victim of other people's unkept promises as well as his own.

"To top it all off," Alan went on, "I just wish when people didn't want to pay or couldn't pay they'd say so rather than pick apart every part of my work. It's amazing how even Christian people believe a good offense is the best defense. They stall and delay payment as if it's a battle. They may owe me ten thousand dollars and they won't release it until some unreasonable demand is met. We are conscientious about our work and will do it over if it's not right, but we're human and there's only so much we can do with concrete and wood.

"You know, I'd much rather work *for* me than *be* me. In times like these," he concluded, "the conscientious manager is shortchanged."

Sound familiar? We can identify with Alan's frustration and anxiety, but there's not a whole lot a Christian brother can do. But is there a legitimate way to alleviate business stresses?

Anxiety ambushes the Christian as well as the non-Christian when there is trouble in an industry, and everyone gets tarred with the same brush. Most of us have heard deprecating remarks such as "How can electricians get that much money for a simple switch?" "All mechanics do now is add parts till the car runs"; "The schools are downright amoral—teachers only want jobs that pay well"; "Government? They're all a bunch of crooks."

To some degree these statements are at once true and false.

Solomon gave an intriguing observation: "Where no oxen are, the crib is clean; but much increase is by the strength of the ox" (Prov. 14:4). Yes, in order to get most jobs done, there is the risk of dirt and disorder. Alan, like many others, got tired of cleaning up someone else's mess and being blamed for it at the same time.

One step toward a solution would be for all of us to refuse to stereotype all members of a group that is irritating us. One day I found myself with a very tense lady on an elevator in the county building. She acted as if she didn't notice me as she murmured over and over, "Please, Jesus, help me." The elevator stopped and the open door revealed a sign with an arrow identifying the floor as the welfare department. I thought of the cruel remarks I've heard about "welfare welchers." What a demeaning thing to sincere people who through no fault of their own need public assistance. The handicapped, the orphaned, the displaced of this industrial society, and many other worthy persons are lumped together with an irresponsible element. How unfair.

This knife cuts both ways. There is no way to escape being in some group—teacher, politician, electrician, used car salesman, Polish, Protestant, black or white, woman or man are all hurt unless we avoid condemning whole groups.

There is more to the group stigma. For some, even competing in the marketplace causes twinges of shame. Numerous young people have dropped out of the business community and retreated to a simple, undemanding life-style. Still others withdraw into a shell to wait for the Lord's return to rescue them from society's swirling forces.

I got a bitter earful from a young man on a trip to the West Coast. As we jetted across the country in the luxury airliner, he lectured me on how corrupt the system had become. Abandoning college, he was flying to a warmer climate where he could escape society's corruption in a remote mountain village. I could appreciate his anguish if he was walking across the country, avoiding the environment-polluting vehicles and subsisting on wild berries. To enjoy the fruits of his father's capitalistic struggles on the way to the simple life carries the taint of hypocrisy.

Risking Bruises in the Marketplace

Several parables in the New Testament deal with our personal behavior and the conduct of our responsibilities. One that touches Alan's problem is the parable of the talents (Matt. 25:14-30).

The "talents" in the parable are not like the talent to play the piano. Rather, they refer to a quantity of money. These men were given money to invest in accordance with their abilities. And notice that the man with five talents is not more important than the man with two or one.

The men went into the marketplace of their day and took the incumbent risks. The man with five talents brought back ten. The man with two brought back four. The third man brought back the one he started with. He had not lost it, but neither had he increased it. I believe this story has much to say to the Alans of the world.

One amazing element in the story is the low estimate the man with one talent had of his master. He thought of him as one who "reaped where he didn't sow" and "gathered where he scattered no seed." The master rebuked the servant, indicating that if he indeed thought him greedy, he should have at least put the money in the bank so it would have earned a little interest.

Every marketplace has risks, and invariably there are dirty places. The only safe, clean way to protect money is to hide it. But the parable tells us the Lord rejects this option. Plainly, the parable commends the marketplace and condemns inactivity and fear.

No conscientious entrepreneur can avoid criticism, misunderstanding, setbacks, and heartaches. Even compromise of his standards will occur through actions beyond his control. The man who pumps gas in a service station is the retail outlet for a multinational company which may be bribing kings, opposing empires, polluting the environment, or corrupting legislators. And the whole enterprise is sustained by customers who use the gasoline. This is one example of the unavoidable compromises in which we are inextricably involved. Some people try to be uninvolved by carefully "burying their talent," then with a sense of naive pride present themselves to the master and brag that they weren't corrupted. But nothing was accomplished either!

We could all wish for simpler ways instead of the complex interdependence of modern life, but most of us cannot go back. Paul's problems with John Mark, John Wesley's marital burdens, Jefferson's writing of the Declaration of Independence while a slave owner, and our Christianity cloaked in our own set of shortcomings have a common thread. We live in a flawed world where progress, not perfection, is possible.

Some Christians, while acknowledging that everyone needs to be saved by grace, act as if their own purity and virtue must not be touched by the world. Such arrogance negates the grace of God in their lives. It renders them impotent in a world which needs Christians to be deeply involved in Christ's work until He returns to make everything right.

Jesus provided the precedent. He talked with an outcast Samaritan woman (John 4:5-43) and recruited a tax collector as His disciple (Luke 5:27). He healed a Roman soldier's servant (Matt. 8:5-13), and was labeled a "winebibber" by critics (11:19). "They that are whole need not a physician, but they that are sick," He explained (Luke 5:31). Doctors in their work risk infection, and Christians serve in a polluted world.

Be Salt

The strategy of the kingdom of God directs that His citizens be spread throughout the earth. Wherever they go, they are not to lose their salt flavoring (Matt. 5:13). A little salt flavors a big roast; and the honest Christian is a potent antidote to evil.

Fidelity rings true in the midst of infidelity, as does sacrifice in the face of selfishness and love in a circle of lust. The salt cannot stay in the saltshaker; the Church must be in the world to accomplish its task. A close brotherhood develops among Christians who strive in an evil world even if they fail perfection. Deep understanding among us is the result of sharing our humanity and the grace of God. It is the essence of the Church. The temptation to retreat from criticism, misunderstanding, and failure is powerful, but the Church is crippled by false expectations of perfection and small confidence in the power of God.

Be Light

The Christian is called to be a light in the world until Christ returns (Matt. 5:14). Today's world is a swamp of relative values, and people need the absolutes of the Word of God. The moral darkness must be illuminated by God's Word lived out in Christian men and women.

Archimedes spoke of a lever, a fulcrum, and a place to stand for moving the world. The solid rock of Jesus Christ is our place to stand for communicating to our society the foundational truths of Scripture.

The world was created by God.

Man was made in the image of God and pronounced "good."

Evil is a destructive intruder.

Man chose to follow evil instead of God.

God revealed His love in Jesus Christ.

Man can be reconciled to God by faith in Christ.

Man is responsible for Earth's management until Christ returns.

Christ will restore justice and righteousness.

These truths are basic, and human history is beyond understanding without them. Christ encourages us to put our light on a hill. What a visible target! When we expose the message of Christ to the world we open ourselves to tremendous personal, societal, and historical questions. People will remind us of hypocrites in the church, the bloody Inquisition and the Crusades of the Middle Ages, the witch burnings and puritanical sexual restrictions of the New World, petty denominational squabbles, and more embarrassing—our own sins. But we must not allow any "basket" to hide the true light of Christ even though it exposes our failings. We walk in the light in order that our deeds may be discerned and by God's grace we are made more serviceable reflectors. Man without Christ has no meaningful past or future. In Christ's light, man can touch God.

Sheep among Wolves

Christians are also as sheep among wolves. The world is often cruel and hostile, but Christians have power to love their enemies and pray for those who despitefully use them (Matt. 5:44). They can walk the second mile and turn the other cheek (5:39-41). In Christ's footsteps, they are servants and ministering priests. All these are losing strategies in the eyes of power-hungry men, but keep in mind that the One who was slain on a cross will return as King of kings and Lord of lords!

The strategy of the Gospel is not a majority attack to take over the world. Rather it's a minority movement that wins individual hearts, minds, and bodies by love. Our weapons are not the weapons of this world, but the winsome powers of truth, forgiveness, and joy.

Be New Centurions

A film entitled "The New Centurions" on TV featured two policemen in a large city—one a rookie, the other a grizzled veteran. The two men risked their lives in the alleys and dives of the city to apprehend burglars and all sorts of unsavory characters. When their shift was finished, they left the police station only to see the men they had arrested already back on the street, released on bail, or dismissed of charges. The policemen comment philosophically about the situation, but feel a sense of futility and defeat.

The rookie wants to quit. "What's the use?" he says.

The veteran policeman asks him, "Have you ever heard of centurions?"

"No," replies the rookie.

"Well," says the veteran, "in early Rome the army was mostly made up of mercenaries and rabble. However, every 100th soldier was a centurion, a committed Roman. He knew where the army was to go, what it was to accomplish, and what their goals were. The centurions kept the army from becoming a mob, and eventually Rome ruled the world. We are the new centurions; we keep the world from tipping into madness."

There is a tremendous truth in this story. The Church of Christ needs every Alan and every other "centurion" to help each other overcome discouragement and defeat and keep moving toward victory. The Christian belongs in the world, not a sheltered fortress. And "where sin abounds grace does much more abound" (see Rom. 5:20; 6:1).

Study Questions
   Read Matthew 25:14-30; 5:13-16; 10:16; Romans 5:20— 6:1; Ephesians 2:8-9.
1. How realistic is it for anyone to try to escape the entanglements of institutions and government?
2. How compromised are Christians in today's society?
3. If you ever were tempted to "drop out" what kept you going?
4. Name some values and benefits the world takes for granted that really come from biblical faith.
5. What does your Christian community offer to men and women compromised or destroyed by the "marketplace"?

6

The Parent-Teen Trauma

I answered the phone and heard a familiar statement: "You don't know us, but after hearing you on the radio and reading your books and articles we feel we know you."

"I'm glad you felt free to call," I said. I meant what I said but I shrank instinctively at the prospect of facing up to another problem.

"We were wondering if we could see you   about a family crisis."

"When would you like to see me?" I said.

"If you're not too busy, we thought perhaps we could come over to your house tonight or maybe you could meet us at your office. We really need help and we don't think it can wait."

"Okay," I said, knowing it wouldn't be just one evening. It never is. "I'll meet you at my office at 7:30."

Ralph and Ann were waiting for me in the driveway. They were a couple in their late 30s or early 40s, seemed successful, drove a late model car and were well-dressed. We went to my office and shared get-acquainted amenities. Then Ann plunged into their urgent story.

"It's our oldest daughter Sue. She's only 15 and we've never had any special problems with her other than the normal things kids face growing up. But a couple of days ago we were completely shocked when the school called and said Sue was caught selling drugs to kids in her class. At first we couldn't believe it, but we know now it's true.

"Sue admits it but doesn't feel it's as big a problem as the school counselors and police made out. She says most of the kids use drugs, not hard stuff, just grass and pills. Now that we've talked about it she feels a little guilty and is sorry we're upset. She says she won't use or sell drugs again.

"The police have been very helpful. They say because of her age and good school record Sue will probably be put on probation in our care. What do you think we should do?"

In this case I suggested they discuss it with their pastor. I asked why they didn't contact him first. "We were afraid he wouldn't understand," they said. As it turned out, he did, and together they worked out their problem.

This kind of problem has become common in churches and families. When it happens, our first response is to reject the idea that this could happen to us, but it is happening in some of the finest homes in the country.

It is interesting to try to discover what happened to the problems in many churches. It appears that members with problems have often felt rejected and in their sense of failure have wandered away from the church. Some have watched this happen to others and hide their own heartaches lest they also get drummed out of the corps.

It's especially hard to deal with problems involving our children. We feel that they are extensions of ourselves and that their faults reflect negatively on us. This shame often compounds the problem by making us defensive or sometimes too uptight to deal objectively with the situation. It is very easy to tell a neighbor or friend to "relax, everything will come out all right," and it's quite another thing when it is our problem.

Facing the Problem

What are some things Christian parents can do when faced with such a situation? Reassurance is very important in times of family crisis. Husbands and wives must affirm their commitment to see it through together. Sometimes one parent will withdraw and let the other struggle with shame, as well as with the child. Admit your feelings to one another and recognize that at different times each will need the other's support.

Another requirement for facing the problem is avoidance of placing blame. Sometimes a family crisis becomes a convenient time to release submerged hostilities and marital resentments. "If you only took more interest in the children, this wouldn't have happened." Our responsibility for young people's actions is shifted to others with the explanation: "Our son is a good boy; it's just our neighborhood"; or "If they would discipline their children, they wouldn't have led ours astray."

Usually there has been no willful neglect by either parent. Blame implies a deliberate wrongdoing, which is rarely the case with parents. It is true that they make many mistakes, and take the wrong course of action in raising their children, but their motives are rarely what is wrong when children get into trouble. Rather than waste time assigning blame, a more positive approach is to forget who is responsible for the family being where it is, and concentrate on what should be done at that moment to start the family on the right course of recovery.

Most situations of this type have complex causes. Even after the storm has passed, you will likely not understand its cause completely. Sometimes we resemble the white mice in a cage that is electrically charged. When the mice are shocked they often attack each other and sometimes even bite themselves. We have the capacity to better identify the problem, but we must always fight the tendency to strike out frantically.

No matter how often we tell our children they are loved, sometimes they will test us to see if our love has conditions attached. Friends may prod: "Of course your parents love you; you do everything they like. Just wait until you do something they disagree with." It's important for your son or daughter to know your love for them is unconditional and unshakable even in the face of disappointment and fear.

Generally in this situation young people argue that "everyone is doing it" and that grass or pills are no more harmful than tobacco or alcohol. Usually they will agree that hard drugs are bad. There are three important aspects to our response.

1. Everyone does not do it. First of all, the teenage use of "everyone" is an inaccurate term and this should be pointed out. Everyone does not use drugs, even if most of the people with whom the teenager associates do. So everybody has not agreed it is all right.

2. It's against the law. As long as drug use is against the law, the practice is wrong no matter what our personal views are. Good citizens are obligated to obey the law unless it is immoral.

3. Three wrongs don't make a right. Third, it is true that alcohol and tobacco are harmful, but "three wrongs don't make a right." Parents who don't use alcohol or tobacco have a stronger argument against drug use than those who indulge.

Parents who are forced to say, "Don't do as I do, do as I say," lose the strong influence of good example.

Data is far from complete on the effects of drug usage. It is not possible to say that any are harmless, and the evidence so far points in the other direction.

A Teenager with a Problem

It's most important that your child understands when you reject his behavior that you accept him. Remember, you do not have a *problem teenager,* you have a *teenager with a problem.* If the person is lost under the problem, no one is left to work with. You must work with the person, not just with the problem.

When a person fails seriously, he can only begin the journey back when he feels trusted. Remember that there was not only a "prodigal son" but a "waiting father" (Luke 15). The waiting, patience, forgiveness, and restoration are all part of that beautiful story.

Sometimes kids say, "What's the use? I make one mistake and I have to start at ground zero. It's as if I never did anything right. Isn't there any credit for the rest of my life?"

They are right, of course. A failure should not mean complete breakdown of trust nor should it trigger parental overreaction to relieve a sense of guilt. Often parents reason, "We've failed so far by being too lax; now we will make up for it by tightening the screws." Grim repression may cause further rebellion that often gets out of hand.

Importance of Self-Respect

Getting into the *why* of a situation may take time and never be entirely clear. Personal and social needs which drive youth and adults to escape through drugs have not been conclusively determined. People often ask me why kids become addicts, and my answer is that we have had the problem of alcoholism for centuries and all of us know drinkers who are not addicted. When we have the answer to alcoholism, we will probably have the answer to drug dependence. We do know that when people experience God's love, learn to accept forgiveness and adopt His goals, they can love themselves and relate healthily to others.

Importance of Accepting Help

Another area of need in these situations is to accept help from fellow Christians. Many church people find it difficult to admit needs and failures. If you are a Christian facing a difficult problem, swallow your egotism and invite some brother or sister to help you "bear your burden" (Gal. 6:2). Giving is often easier than receiving, as we like to be strong and help others. Rugged individualism is an unrealistic and unspiritual way to live. Good receivers make better givers next time around; through this process we learn to "love one another."

Peter would have found it easier to wash Jesus' feet than have his feet washed by Jesus. Such pride makes us like castles with moats and drawbridges raised. It is only when we lower the bridge and allow others to know and help us that true fellowship begins.

If you know someone in a place of difficulty, offer to be of help. "A friend loveth at all times, and a brother is born for adversity" (Prov. 17:17). It will thrill you to discover how much help is given by serving one another in prayer and caring concern.

Importance of Discussion

It is often useful to invite other parents with teens to share your experience and discuss how these problems develop and possible strategies to use in the midst of them. Others may have tried something that will work for you. Prayer and support of each other will be of great help. Don't be afraid to invite non-Christians to such a meeting. Your openness and desire to give and receive help will be a witness of Christ to them. A caring community is unusual in today's world and most people are hungry for it.

Many families think the best strategy when a problem develops is to get a lid on it, then sit on the lid and pretend nothing is wrong. This shuts us off from one of the greatest opportunities for Christian growth—that of receiving love and ministry from others. Paul tells us to "rejoice with them that do rejoice, and weep with them that weep" (Rom. 12:15).

Importance of Forgiveness

Most drug problems today are "growing-up" problems and will be forgotten like other youthful problems of the past. Some are more serious and will bring heartache or ruin, leaving scars that never quite heal. This type requires competent professional counseling, and some will defy solution. In any case, a forgiving spirit supported by love and affirmation creates a good climate for healing.

Christians who share their defeats and victories in the supportive fellowship of believers build strong defenses against the Enemy of our souls.

Study Questions

Read Job 2:11-13; Proverbs 17:17; Romans 12:15; Galatians 6:2; Matthew 11:28-30; Proverbs 11:14; 2 Corinthians 1:4.

1. What has happened to Christians you know who have put the "lid" on some boiling problems?
2. If you sought help for personal needs, would you find it in your church?

3. What are some things parents can do if a teenager is unrepentant and insists on disobeying?
4. How can parents demonstrate trust in young people?
5. What are some difficulties in "separating the sin from the sinner"?
6. What factors make the "yoke easy and the burden light"?
7. What values could come from the silent waiting of Job 2:11-13?

7

Second-class Christians

Jim and Martha have lived all their lives in a wealthy suburb of a large northern city. While Jim is active in his local church, he dislikes speaking in public, so avoids teaching a Sunday School class or sharing his testimony in a church meeting. His main claim to fame is that he has a good business sense and is trusted with projects and board responsibilities.

Jim could have retired because his children are grown and his business is now largely in the hands of capable managers. However, he chose to go into semi-retirement and to spend each morning with Martha enjoying a relaxed breakfast and devotional time. It was partly this practice of lingering over breakfast and Bible reading which created a new problem.

One of the often-overlooked details in Jim's business was to arrange for someone to clean up and haul away construction debris. This detail could easily have been assigned to someone else, but Jim took it as his assignment. It gave him a sense of involvement.

The man Jim hired for this job was a black man named

Pete who with his son ran a general hauling business. When Pete came to Jim's back door to receive his instructions, Jim often invited him in for a cup of coffee. Their conversation was always cordial, and soon, because of Jim's open Bible, Jim and Pete discovered they shared the same personal faith in Jesus Christ.

Both men were about the same age, both had grown children, both were devoted husbands, and both were active in their churches. Often their discussion went beyond the limits of business arrangements, and soon a comfortable rapport developed between them. More than once they ended their visit with prayer and often promised to visit each other's church "to get better acquainted." It was more polite than specific, like the invitation, "You ought to visit us sometime."

And then it happened. Local newspapers began to feature articles about the volatile busing issue. People began choosing sides and feelings erupted, even in Jim's Sunday School class. Jim spoke up about his relationship with Pete and tried to dispel the myth of black stereotypes. A local white minister came into prominence as a spokesman against "outside agitators" who were trying to upset the normally tranquil community.

At the height of the furor Pete called and said, "Jim, what time does your service begin tomorrow."

"Eleven o'clock," said Jim.

"Good," said Pete. "My son, Pete Jr., and myself are planning to come to your service tomorrow and I thought we could sit together."

Immediately Jim thought of the biased views some of his friends had expressed in the Sunday School class. To his knowledge, no black person had attended their services, except a visiting black choir which had traded services with their own on a special Sunday a few years previously. Jim didn't want to get caught in the middle of a battle or lose his reputation as a dependable businessman, but he knew things must change.

"OK," he said after a lengthy pause. "Let's meet in front of the church at 10:45 A.M. so we can get a good seat." Jim's plan was to arrive early and be seated before most of the congregation arrived.

But Pete and his son did not arrive until 11 o'clock. The meditation was over and they waited for the choir to finish before being seated. As the usher led them down the aisle to seats near the front, Jim wondered what his friends were thinking.

After the service Jim was happy with the generally friendly atmosphere. Pete was relaxed and cordial and many people introduced themselves. Jim and Martha said good-bye to their guests and returned to greet some friends they had missed. But as they reentered the church they overheard someone say, "I wonder what they're trying to prove? Things like this shouldn't be forced." When people saw Jim and Martha the conversation halted. One man, a friend of many years, turned away and left without a word.

"Since that day," related Jim and Martha when they came to see me, "we've felt rejected in our church. It seemed impossible that prejudice like this could happen in our mission-oriented church. Frankly, we're hurt and confused. We don't know what we should do."

This true experience is being repeated in various ways today and is a challenge to many Christians. The troubled '60s have passed, yet many like Jim and Martha still face unresolved racial problems and desire a realistic faith to confront them.

There is no question that many churches have become involved in attempting to solve social inequities and consequently have been split into factions. Others have lost their

Gospel perspective and have forgotten the message of personal salvation. Many conclude that if one dimension of the Gospel must be neglected it is serious to minimize the social. Equally sincere people cannot see the relevance of the message unless it affects the way we live. The pendulum has swung between faith and works until some have imagined a disagreement between the writings of Paul and James on the issue. Many evangelical leaders have written books and articles on the Christian social responsibility, and yet few individuals or churches want to touch the issues that almost tore apart the nation in the '60s.

The real question is: What does the Bible say on the issue? Is there any precedent in Scripture to guide us in our situation?

Despised Samaritans

According to the fourth chapter of John, Jesus faced a situation similar to Jim and Martha's. About noon one day, after a long, hot journey, Jesus came across a Samaritan woman drawing water from a well. The Jews despised the Samaritans and wouldn't even speak to them. Jesus could have hung back and waited for the woman to finish and then get His own water, but He didn't, and we have one the most poignant stories in all Scripture.

It might seem unnecessarily provocative for Jesus to make a Samaritan the heroine of His story, especially when He was aware of the racial tensions between Jews and Samaritans. Why not use a good Jew to illustrate the important truth of genuine worship? Doubtless the reason was that critical problems are not solved until they are "brought to the surface" and confronted.

We might ask if one incident is enough to impel us into situations that are difficult and almost certain to be divisive. The same observations we have made about the woman at the well are also true of the story of the Good Samaritan. Why a good *Samaritan?* Why not a good Jew? We know that there were thousands of them, but Jesus forces us into the situation because of its importance. Keep in mind that He is dealing with people chosen to carry His message of life to the world. They had allowed nationalistic pride to smother the message of faith given by Abraham. They had forgotten that God was on their side in days of old because of their faithfulness, not because of their race. Racial superiority is foreign and hateful to the heart of Jesus Christ.

All Are Precious

Many generous, gracious Christians have never had a public test of their faith. It is one thing to see missionary slides of cute African children and then pray lovingly about their needs. It is quite another to face racial problems in our community or church after generations of neglect and prejudice.

Emotions easily flare when we discuss racial or women's rights. Some say, "These issues are not part of the Church. We should stick to the Gospel!" But the Gospel says that all people are to be offered the love and redemption of God, and prejudice of all kinds is condemned in God's Word. The children sing, "Red and yellow, black and white, all are precious in His sight," and then grow up to find a different theology being lived. Surely one of the fiercest tests of God's love in Christians is our response to racial differences.

Something deep within us often says, "Let sleeping dogs lie." But is this the voice of God? Perhaps a sleeping dog should be caged while we plan strategies for the confrontation that's sure to come. Take my word for it—this issue is no longer "sleeping."

Throughout the Old and New Testaments God is the Friend and Protector of the poor and oppressed. There is a consistent equation in Scripture between righteousness and the way we treat the poor and weak. Personal godliness identifies with disenfranchised people as well as with pious attitudes

Biblical Integrity

Many Christians urge us to "leave well enough alone," saying these divisive issues blunt the sword of evangelism. In Scripture we find the Early Church dealing promptly with any issue which threatened to make a hypocrisy of the Gospel message. James spoke out against class distinctions (2:1-10); Paul insisted on Peter's social integrity in relation to the Gentiles (Gal. 2:11-14); and Paul pleaded, "Let [your] love be without hypocrisy" (Rom. 12:9, NASB). The early Christians realized they could not prove God's love to a skeptical world if they did not live it. The stresses of spiritual growing pains are preferable to the cancers of hypocrisy and hatred which corrupt the Christian body and cripple evangelism.

I am convinced that the enduring appeal of Negro spirituals is the composers' intuitive realization that Jesus understands the travail of His people. He will right the wrongs and punish the oppressor. One does not need to be a theologian to recognize the truth of this message. When people see the Church lining up with Christ on these issues without excluding the saving message of the Cross, they must acknowledge its integrity and reality.

The priesthood of the believer implies ministry on behalf of other people. The writer of Hebrews made a case for Christ's priesthood on the basis of His "sharing the same blood and flesh" we possess. He became "like His brethren" so that He might become a merciful and faithful High Priest (see Heb. 2:14-18).

With Him as our example, we must identify with the needs of others. This lending of our equity to others is one way in which we reconcile the world to God. This is the social equivalent of cosigning a loan for someone. Sometimes we can take some of the respect, influence, and reputation which we have built up over the years and risk some of it for a weaker brother. Jesus was criticized for His identification with Zaccheus (Luke 19:5-7). Without the reflected respectability of Jesus upon him, Zaccheus might not have felt the love of God in his life.

There is an interesting relationship in the judgment passage in Matthew 25:31-45:

When the Son of man shall come in His glory, and all the holy angels with Him, then shall He sit upon the throne of His glory;

And before Him shall be gathered all nations, and He shall separate them one from another, as a shepherd divideth his sheep from the goats.

And He shall set the sheep on His right hand, but the goats on the left.

Then shall the King say unto them on His right hand, "Come, ye blessed of My Father, inherit the kingdom prepared for you from the foundation of the world.

"For I was an hungered, and ye gave Me meat; I was thirsty, and ye gave Me drink; I was a stranger, and ye took me in;

"Naked, and ye clothed Me; I was sick, and ye visited Me; I was in prison, and ye came unto Me."

Then shall the righteous answer Him, saying, "Lord, when saw we Thee an hungered, and fed Thee? Or thirsty, and gave Thee drink?

"When saw we Thee a stranger, and took Thee in? Or naked, and clothed Thee?

"Or when saw we Thee sick, or in prison, and came unto Thee?"

And the King shall answer and say unto them, "Verily I say unto you, inasmuch as ye have done it unto one of the least of these My brethren, ye have done it unto Me."

Then shall He say also unto them on the left hand, "Depart from Me, ye cursed, into everlasting fire, prepared for the devil and his angels.

"For I was an hungered, and ye gave Me no meat; I was thirsty, and ye gave Me no drink; I was a stranger, and ye took Me not in; naked, and ye clothed Me not; sick, and in prison, and ye visited Me not."

Then shall they also answer Him, saying, "Lord, when saw we Thee an hungered, or athirst, or a stranger, or naked, or sick, or in prison, and did not minister unto Thee?"

Then shall He answer them, saying, "Verily I say unto thee, inasmuch as ye did it not to one of the least of these, ye did it not to Me."

And these shall go away into everlasting punishment; but the righteous into life eternal.

Notice the identification of Jesus with the hungry, thirsty, naked, the strangers, and the prisoners who believe in Him: "Inasmuch as you have done it unto one of the least of these My brethren, yet have done it unto Me." We love Him when we love His people of all conditions. Likewise, to neglect one of these is to neglect Him.

There are major principles here that an honest, growing Christian cannot ignore.

1. Barriers between people are broken down by the love and power of Jesus Christ, and they must be overcome by His Church.

2. Faithful Christians, like Christ Himself, must identify with the needy of the world and bridge the various gaps to touch our fellowmen for Christ.

3. We will be tried according to our loving deeds as well as words at the final judgment.

Study Questions

Read James 2:1-4; Acts 10:25; Galatians 2:11-14; Romans 12:9; Hebrews 2:14; 4:15; 5:2; 9:28; Matthew 9:11; John 4:4-30; Luke 10:33; Matthew 25:31-45.

1. How do evangelism and social responsibilities relate to each other?
2. How can the church help resolve racial alienation?
3. Describe individual acts of charity and institutional policies that have healed racial stress.
4. In what ways are Christians better prepared than nonbelievers to deal with inequalities?
5. If racial prejudice does not come from God and the Bible, what is its source?

8

God Gave,
Jesus Gave, I . . .

It has always amazed me how some Christians with few resources manage to be so faithful in their giving. After a church appeal for special funds when I was project treasurer, a couple handed me a sizable check. Later as another need came before the church, another pledge came from the same couple. Knowing the man had small children and had been out of work, I wondered how they could give such a substantial amount.

An opportunity arose one day to discuss finances with this couple and they shared their story with me. When they were first married, they illustrated the curious economic rule that "expenses rise to meet income." Nancy confronted Bill after work one day and said, "Are you aware that our family finances are in absolute shambles?" This was followed by his accusations about her not being able to handle money. She countered with defensive remarks about how she did her best but he was too impulsive and constantly threw their checkbook into disarray. Since Bill disliked unpleasantness, he let the matter drop, hoping that the problem would work out "somehow."

Later at a sharing time in the church, someone told how they had been blessed by tithing their income. Bill and Nancy didn't know what the word "tithe" meant and in embarrassment asked one of the other couples. "When we learned it referred to the promise that Jacob made to give one-tenth of all he possessed, it really amazed us," said Bill. "We went home and talked about how we had asked Christ to help us in every other area of our lives but somehow had overlooked the spending of money. Our assumption had been that the church got sufficient money from the different offerings. We decided to study the Bible to see what was there for us on this subject. We didn't see how we could give 10% immediately, but decided to turn it over to God and see what happened."

"What have you learned?" I asked.

"Lots of things," said Bill. "First we learned that giving is a matter of resolve. That is, you must decide what you're going to do and do it. If you wait until everything else is paid and all you want is bought, you'll never have anything left. We now give our tithe off the top, save 10% off the bottom, and live on what's in between."

"We've also learned," added Nancy, "that if you can't give of your little, you probably won't give when you have a lot. It's a matter of commitment."

"Another thing we've learned is that you get more than you give," Bill said. "Somehow nine-tenths goes farther than ten-tenths. Don't ask us how it works, it just does and we no longer have the same crises we used to have over money."

Since talking with Bill and Nancy, I've discussed this matter with many couples and found the testimonials to be approximately the same. All agree that when they start with a tithe priority, other priorities are easier to establish. Perhaps this accounts for the nine-tenths going farther than the ten-tenths.

Give as You've Been Given

There's enough said in the Bible about giving to show that money involves more than economics. Money, in fact, seems to be a tangible symbol of where our "heart" is. In 2 Corinthians 8—9, the connection is made concerning Christ— "Do you remember the generosity of Jesus Christ, the Lord of us all? He was rich, yet He became poor for your sakes so that His poverty might make you rich" (8:9, PH), and in his letter to the Roman Christians, Paul said that one who has received spiritual blessings should give monetary gifts.

The word "stewardship" is often used in the New Testament in relation to Christian responsibility. Unfortunately, we use this word almost exclusively in relationship to fund drives. The concept of true stewardship is that all that we have: life, talent, energy, influence, and resource are given to us in trust by God.

The teaching of Paul on spiritual and natural gifts is consistent with this concept. What we possess is not the result of our superior effort and self-made opportunities, but comes to us from God to be used for His purposes in the world. This trust is much like the arrangement we have with our bank. We deposit money for safekeeping and for profit. The bank officers make decisions that allow them to return interest to us and still provide profit for the bank. If you went to your bank to withdraw your funds and the banker refused to give them to you, he would no longer be a steward but a thief. This is a fairly accurate illustration of our relationship to God.

This truth is pivotal for Christians. Until we accept it we are unable to given any resource in the proper spirit. Many give without this understanding, and the faulty spirit produces resentment, greed, and attempts to manipulate and obligate others. To the elder boy in the parable of the Prodigal Son, the father expresses his stewardship: "My child, you have always been with me, and all that is mine is yours" (Luke 15:31, NASB).

Give When Led

Second, there is a "grace" connected with giving. It will never surface in our lives, however, until we understand and accept the role of steward. So long as we hang on to the ownership of our lives and grasp our resources as our own property, it will be a painful process to give them to anyone. They will have to be pried from us by obligation, guilt, or pride. God desires that we understand this principle behind the phrase, "Ye are not your own; ye are bought with a price" (1 Cor. 6:20).

The churches in Macedonia had this grace even though they were in poverty. "And now, brothers, we want you to know about the grace that God has given the Macedonian churches. Out of the most severe trial, their overflowing joy and their extreme poverty welled up in rich generosity" (2 Cor. 8:1-2, NIV). Notice the progression of their giving in subsequent verses: they gave themselves to God, then to other churches, then begged Paul for the favor of participating in the "service to the saints" (see 8:3-5).

This voluntary giving or grace from God was Paul's desire for the Corinthians (2 Cor. 9:7). He was so anxious for them to be led by the Holy Spirit and not feel intimidated by his presence that he asked for the offering to be taken before he arrived (1 Cor. 16:1-2; 2 Cor. 9:5). One can be critical of financial drives using leverage of personal influence, competition and guilt, but till the principles of grace are understood and applied, these worldly methods will be used. And the world then misses the marvel of true Christian charity.

Give Abundantly

There is a third principle connected with this subject. Paul says a person's gift should not be measured by its size but by what the giver keeps. "And here is my advice about what is best for you in this matter: Last year you were the first not only to give but also to have the desire to do so. Now finish the work, so that your eager willingness to do it may be matched by your completion of it, according to your means. For if the willingness is there, the gift is acceptable according to what a man has, not according to what he does not have. Our desire is not that others might be relieved while you are hard pressed, but that there might be equality. At the present time your plenty will supply what they need, so that in turn their plenty will supply what you need. Then there will be equality, as it is written: 'He that gathered much did not have too much, and he that gathered little did not have too little' " (8:10-15, NIV).

Both illustrations argue that we have an obligation to look at our abundance and also at how much we keep. Paul argues for a reciprocal sharing wherever abundance confronts need.

"From each according to his ability, to each according to his need" is a despised phrase flaunted by the Communist theorists. Never more than a slogan, it should be the basis of voluntary charity practiced by newborn individuals who have transferred ownership to the Lord Jesus.

Give Voluntarily

The voluntary giving of Christians recorded in Acts 4:32 and 5:1-2 indicates this principle was preached in the churches not only by Paul, but by Peter and John as well. In all instances, voluntary giving is stressed. When giving is the result of pressure, obligation, or guilt, the negatives often outweigh the value of the gift. Under these circumstances the giver receives no joy or reward. He feels only resentment and a sense of having been violated by external pressure. Christian giving should be born of a deep sense of gratitude to God for His "unspeakable gift" (2 Cor. 9:15), from a humble heart which acknowledges that every good and perfect gift comes from God (James 1:17), and that our abilities and all we possess are gifts from Him (Rom. 12).

This voluntary principle applies in other areas of our lives as well. One can easily identify with the mother who reminds her children in subtle ways that Mother's Day is approaching, and when she does receive gifts she wonders if they were really motivated by love or obligation caused by her coercion. She has the gifts all right, but it was the love she wanted. Love is clearly a voluntary relationship. "God so loved that He gave . . ." (John 3:16).

Responsible Administration
Where should we give our gifts? Many of the Old Testament verses on tithes and offerings and some offerings mentioned in Acts relate to needs presently met by taxes. Social welfare was unknown in ancient cultures. Paul speaks of the necessity for church integrity in the administration of these donations (2 Cor. 9:12). It's interesting to note that the New Testament offerings were spent for the welfare of the needy in the church and for the support of missionaries and evangelists when necessary.

It is possible to have ecclesiastical greed—the desire to control others through the collected money of God's people (James 4:3). Men and women with gifts of administration are needed to assure the most effective use of His resources.

The truth of "a penny saved is a penny earned" applies to the Church as well as the individual even in inflated economics.

Givers and Takers

One final note will encourage us when we suspect the recipients of our help do not use the funds as wisely as we would like. We sometimes give to individuals or agencies and are disappointed in the disposition of our offering. The bright side of this is that the giving in God's name brings the benefit and reward. The receiver can burn the money for a weiner roast and not rob the giver of his blessing. Keep in mind that the Old Testament sacrifices went up in smoke! Society might be divided into two classes—the givers and the takers, and we are told "God loves a cheerful giver"! (2 Cor. 9:7)

Study Questions

Read 2 Corinthians 8—9; Romans 15:25-27; Acts 11:29-30; Acts 4:32; 5:11; James 4:3; Luke 19:8; Proverbs 11:25; 28:27; Luke 18:12; Matthew 23:23; Genesis 28:22.

1. Describe some specific spiritual blessings that have come from giving.
2. In view of the tax burden for social welfare, is a tithe too great for Christian givers?
3. Can you confirm a relationship between giving and success in real life?
4. When expenses rise to meet income, what are some alternatives?
5. How does the principle of voluntary giving square up with Paul's specific requests for help to needy churches?
6. What attitudes sometimes betray our belief that success is related to our abilities rather than the grace of God?
7. Could a Christian ever give away "too much"? Why or why not?

9

Stress Strengthened This Family

"They are one of the most devoted families I know," a friend said about George and Carol and their children. In view of the fragmentation of modern families, it was reassuring to hear they aren't all on the verge of collapse. I wondered what special gifts George and Carol had that lifted them above the average.

I talked with George and Carol, expecting to receive the kind of advice you'd get from an octogenarian when asked the secret of his long life—some formula to cheat old age. Instead, I found Carol a little embarrassed that I should ask. "With company transfers and George changing sales jobs," said Carol, "it's a wonder we made it at all. Looking back, I think we put quite a strain on our family."

"How many times have you moved?" I asked.

"We once added it up and found we've moved 15 times in 26 years of marriage. In addition, George has always traveled."

Their story made me think of the many teenagers I've met who feel insecure and resentful over family moves and have retreated into their shells through fear of making new friends and facing strange situations.

When you ask a husband and wife for the secret of their family stability, most have difficulty verbalizing it. Yet I've found interesting similarities as I've analyzed families where children grow up with happy childhood memories, a healthy sense of independence, respect for their parents, and appreciation for their parents' ethical and religious value systems.

Old-fashioned Love

First, the husband and wife are committed to each other. Their act is together, and the kids know it. The children know they were conceived by a mother and father who are in love with each other, and contrary to whatever may seem chic, cosmopolitan, or "in," this love is manifested by loyalty and fidelity. They also respect each other.

The children know their parents do not seek advantage by putting each other down, nor do they seek to look superior at the other's expense. A son or daughter finds it difficult, if not impossible, to forgive one parent for destroying the other's self-esteem. Husbands or wives who display superiority by constantly correcting each other on minor points or who ignore each other in public always lose in the eyes of their children. The ultimate put-down is sexual infidelity. Boys find it difficult to forgive their fathers for unfaithfulness to their mothers. The same thing generally holds for daughters with a mother's waywardness. They expect much of their own parents even if they argue differently among their friends or if society settles for less.

The man is not "cock of the roost" in the happy home. And the wife is not secretly using a womanly-weakness ploy to manipulate her husband. Rather, they are man and woman who have accepted their roles as gifts from God. They defer to one another from the strength of their persons, not unwillingly out of obligation.

Mutual Respect

Second, the wife is committed to the importance of her husband's work, and he respects his wife as an equal. Many churches are divided over this issue. Some feminists have overstated their case, and, unfortunately, some of their leaders' personalities send chills down the spines of men. This is like throwing down the gauntlet to defenders of male leadership. If they happen to be Christians, they will often pull a biblical arrow from the writings of Paul and wing it home to end the argument. A careful reading of Scripture on the subject, however, will yield a balance that few of us have practiced.

When George is away from home, Carol tries to support what he is doing as worthwhile and necessary. She tells the children that they and she should be grateful that their father works hard and provides for their needs. He is turn is supportive of her role.

Perhaps no one has faced the problem of mobility more than those in the armed forces. The military has studied the problem of mobility and discovered the single most important factor for family stability is the wife's support of her husband's work. If she feels he is performing valuable service to his country and conveys this to the children, they grow up happy and well-adjusted with a minimum of rebellion. If on the other hand the mother constantly complains about her husband being underpaid, underappreciated, and calls down the government because it doesn't know what it's doing, the children will "catch" her discontentment and display antisocial behavior.

One could lament the inequities of modern life and the demands on our families, but the need is to counteract these with positive actions and attitudes. A husband who feels his family appreciates his work will be more joyful and desirous to make his time at home pleasant and creative. Likewise, fathers must convey to wife and children that "sticking by the stuff" at home is not secondary but vital to the well-being of the whole family. When he shares these home tasks, he shows the family that they are important. The idea of "women's work," derided by a superior male, has done terrible damage to the home. A man whose masculinity does not need machismo symbols to cloak his fears will encourage his wife to support his actual needs.

Growing Together

A third characteristic of healthy families is that all members know that family concerns have priority. This is conveyed in a number of almost inconspicuous ways. George always calls Carol when he is on the road and makes a point of talking to each child. I remember hearing one young father burning up dimes on a pay phone one night as he asked his small son, "How does a doggy go? How does a chicky go? How does a kitty go?" This was probably the best use a dime ever got! Families realize when they are first in their fathers' minds.

Further, George always takes the first flight out even if it means arriving home in the small hours of the morning. Carol knows his heart is with her. "I give my work all I have during the week," said George, "but give the weekends to my family."

An evening at a ball game, scout meeting, or concert at the local school will express effective sermons on love. The drives back and forth to school and church are appreciated (and noticed) even if no verbal thanks comes from a too-busy teenager's vocal cords. If wives, children, or husbands do not have a place of primacy in the home, they may go elsewhere for attention or attract attention through bizarre behavior. I've noticed that our collie dog will walk all the way across the yard for a pat on the head—I'm a lot like that, and I suspect you are too.

Strong Church Life

With each move to a new location, George and Carol's first quest was a house near a good church.

"What is a good church?" I asked them.

"We're interested in a church where the emphasis is on Bible-based teaching and preaching," said George. "Interesting sermons and warmhearted services are a factor, but sound doctrine is foundational. I'm also concerned that a local church display a positive atmosphere and practice love."

Carol elaborated about a bad choice they made in one city where the church was nationally known with a famous preacher, but where a spirit of criticism prevailed. "We knew something was wrong," she said, "but were not sure at first what it was. The kids noticed it first and said, 'They know what *not* to do, but not what *to* do.' We were afraid we would catch their problem."

"What else?" I probed.

"The church should believe in families and encourage family life," said Carol. "Some of our church friends are closer than family relatives. They're one of life's greatest gifts! The church can fulfill its role in our mobile culture by giving our families surrogate uncles, aunts, grandmas, and grandfathers."

Consistent Discipline

"Another essential trait in families," George added, "is that fathers accept their responsibility to discipline—even after a hard day of work! It shouldn't all be left to our wives. The good guy-bad guy reputation is not fair to anyone."

It is very tough to separate discipline from our feelings. Let's face it, sometimes we get angry, sometimes we don't have opportunity for a reasoned answer—and we explode rather than correct a child. Unpredictable parental response makes insecure children. Not knowing what to expect or what behavior is rewardable breaks down the personality. Parents must make special efforts to help each other with these failings, not work against each other to the detriment of everyone.

Talk It Over
Not many of us enjoy surprise decisions which disrupt our normal procedures. Successful families look for ways to discuss forthcoming changes. An unexplained announcement from Dad involving a family move, cancelled vacation, or tightened budget will generate no enthusiasm. Sitting down together and laying out the change or crisis will encourage understanding and cooperation. One family I know allows their teenagers to manage the family checkbook for a month at a time. This is good preparation for a family budget discussion. Family members may not always agree or be able to accept change without some pain, but if they have time to think of positive as well as negative aspects and wrestle with the alternatives, any necessary changes can be accomplished with much less resentment and hurtful reaction.

Applying God's Word
The mobile society and demands upon the breadwinner are not going to slow down. The vigorous competitiveness of the marketplace will continue to drain away energy, time, and emotions. Can those who lived in Bible times, living by daylight hours, and traveling at the pace of running horse or camel, help members of a jet-age society manipulated by industrial psychologists stimulating their psyche with subliminal motivators?

It is interesting to note that the patriarch Abraham was called by God to a traveling life (Gen. 12:1-3; Heb. 11:9). Deuteronomy 6 lays out a pattern for religious education for a family on the move. Keep in mind that these people had never seen a religious book or Christian film and had no family counseling centers. The close family ties were created by a chosen life-style—a commitment to an authority structure given them by God.

"More is caught than taught." This true statement is illustrated by youth workers who involve teenagers in stress camping. The stress experience uses controlled conditions—the mountain climbing, hiking, bicycling, or camping to reproduce aspects of life struggles.

Family life in modern society has many stresses. Parents, like youth workers, can make these positive and negative experiences sources of Christian education.

We often read of Old Testament patriarchs moving according to the needs of their flocks. Though their life was nomadic, it was also tribal. Fathers and their brothers, their brothers-in-law and their families, cast their lot together. They shared problems with each other, talked around a camp fire, and demonstrated their faith in the dynamics of daily life. There were critical choices, successes, and failures, but these produced the heroes of faith.

Someone said, "The best defense is a good offense." This is true for today's mobile, demanding society. The family of God will continue to produce success models as we accept, apply and establish the principles of Scripture in our daily living.

Study Questions

Read Genesis 12:1-8; 13:1-18; Deuteronomy 6:4-7; Hebrews 11:9.

1. What are some similarities between nomadic Israel and modern corporate life?
2. What can we learn from biblical tribal life for contemporary church relationships?
3. What are some alternatives to mobility?
4. As perceived by children, how can love between parents be seen?
5. What are ways in which your family has become aware of their priority in your concerns?
6. Contrast the family repercussions when a surprise decision was announced and when discussion revealed a major change.

10

The Couple Who Could Forget

I had been the guest speaker at a church in the Southeast, and the pastor had arranged for me to go home after the service with a young married couple. As they were new Christians, he thought I might be able to encourage them. In the narthex the pastor introduced me to the husband, a shy young man who looked uncomfortable in his Sunday suit. The pastor explained that after Bill got out of the Navy, he settled down, married, and began an apprenticeship as a steam fitter.

When we got to the car, Bill introduced me to his wife Becky and their four-year-old daughter Ann. I had been away from home for several days and missed my own daughters, so I welcomed the opportunity to climb in the back seat with their little girl.

On the way home Becky seemed nervous but I ignored it, knowing that having "the preacher" for dinner no doubt put her under a strain. I wished she would relax and enjoy the fellowship, as I prefer going home with a family to eating alone in a hotel.

Many cooks seem to think pastors and evangelists are silos to be filled to the brim, and that the current meal is the one to do it! So most hostesses overdo on the food, and I could sense Becky was not going to be outdone. But she began by announcing she was not an experienced cook and they weren't used to having important people for dinner.

I searched for some way to relax the hosts and decided to take off my suit coat. As I rolled up my shirt sleeves and loosened my tie, Bill took advantage of the opportunity to remove his jacket. "That feels better," he said. "I always feel so restricted in my suit. I think that's why I sometimes have trouble staying awake in church!"

Little Ann was the only one who looked relaxed. She began to tell me about her kitty and asked if my children had one. Then, changing the subject, she asked, "Do you always talk that loud when you're up there in front?" This added to Becky's discomfort, though not mine. I commented on their lovely new house and Bill said, "We moved in this January just after we got married." I didn't have to calculate that January to August was not long enough to have a four-year-old, but assumed they were remarried or that Becky was widowed.

The meal was delicious, and as Becky sensed Bill's pride and my delight, she began to relax and smile in a reserved way. After the dessert, Ann ran to find her kitty and Bill said, "I suppose you wonder how we happen to have a four-year-old daughter."

I was unprepared for his remark but said, "No, not really. There are lots of possible answers."

Becky moved closer to Bill and he took her hand as he said, "We're both glad for our church and pastor and what God has done for us." He obviously wanted to share something but seemed troubled.

Since he took a strong lead, I encouraged: "Tell me about it."

"When I was in the Navy I was stationed here. Navy towns and sailors are pretty rough, and I did just about everything you could imagine. One night I got crying drunk and began to feel sad, guilty, and sorry for myself. I was out wandering around when I heard preaching in the church we now attend. I went in and sat at the back, hoping no one would notice I was drunk.

"After the service people were friendly and invited me to come downstairs and have coffee and cake in the fellowship hall. I appreciated their acceptance of me and started to attend services. I soon joined the choir and enjoyed everything. It reminded me of home.

"I'd been at the church for a few weeks when one of the women brought a friend. It was Becky." At this point he looked at Becky for a nod of approval and seemed to squeeze her hand a little tighter. "Well, as you can see, she's pretty! She kept coming and as we were both in choir I got to know her and her daughter, Ann, who came with her to choir practice.

"It wasn't long before I wanted to get to know her better and I inquired to see if she was married. When I learned she wasn't, I asked her out. She was good at making excuses, but she finally capitulated and we started dating.

"One night I asked Becky about Ann. Without hesitating she looked straight into my eyes and said, 'Have you ever been to the Flamingo Bar?' I told her I had. 'Well,' she said, 'I work there. I'm a bar girl and a little more, too.' I guess she thought that would scare me off but I laughed and said, 'Wouldn't those people in the choir be surprised if they knew what we know?'

"I went on to explain that my life hadn't been all that clean either, but we could forget our pasts and start all over with Christ. It took a lot of persuading, but we were finally able to turn it over to Christ and begin a whole new life together, and it's been great!" The way they looked at each other, the simplicity and purity of their trust in Christ, their practice of grace together made me realize my pastor friend had wanted me to have one of the great experiences of a lifetime.

The Early Church must have been like that. No pretense. Everyone knew what everyone once was. In fact, Paul often reminded them to keep them from spiritual pride, the kind that forgets what Christ has done and excludes others from the grace of God and power of forgiveness. What a wonderful thing when people learn that forgiveness means forgetting.

A common criticism of Christ's ministry was that He spent His time with sinners. The same was true of the Early Church, so much so in fact that some accused them of being only rabble.

It interested me a few years ago when a song called "The Harper Valley P.T.A." became an overnight hit. The song is the story of how some people critical of the way a woman was raising her daughter recoiled when she came to the P.T.A. meeting and told all of the hidden sins of the community leaders.

What's the appeal of this kind of song?

I think it strikes a universal chord inside people. Most people I know have a dislike for hypocrisy and love to see it put down.

As you talk to people outside the church, one of the first criticisms is that there are hypocrites in the church. Christians profess one thing and practice another. I suspect, however, the accusation often arises because people who have sinned publicly have never publicly acknowledged the forgiveness of Christ. Many early Christians were notorious sinners, but their open acknowledgement of the power of Christ let the world know their new status.

Failure to acknowledge our past sins may keep people from Christ. There is no one to expose when Christians openly glorify Christ for His forgiveness. When sinners are accepted as potential saints, doors of communication are opened.

Too often this forgiving, forgetting spirit is missing in the Church. For this we are often called "holier than thou," "hypocrites" or "phony." The needy often stay away from the church that seems to welcome only the "good people."

Second-Class Scouts
Since that afternoon with Bill and Becky I've met many Christians who have managed to get past Christ's inspection but still feel unforgiven by Christians. Some feel as if they've joined a Boy Scout troop rather than the Church of Jesus Christ. Their past failures keep them forever as second-class scouts—unqualified to teach Sunday School or hold administrative offices. It must delight Satan to see the grace of God made of less effect than the rigorous requirements of some church leaders. This is the opposite of the invitation of Christ who says, "Come unto Me, all ye that labor and are heavy laden, and I will give you rest" (Matt. 11:28). One wonders how the Enemy of our souls convinces so many that sins are on a color wheel: the grays and off-whites at one end—gossip, lying, laziness, slander—and at the other, robbery, murder, and sexual sin.

In 1 Corinthians 6:9-11 we're shown the kind of people which composed the church in Corinth. "Those who live immoral lives, who are idol worshipers, adulterers, or homosexuals—will have no share in His kingdom. Neither will thieves or greedy people, drunkards, slanderers, or robbers. There was a time when some of you were just like that but now your sins are washed away, and you are set apart for God, and He has accepted you because of what the Lord Jesus Christ and the Spirit of our God have done for you" (LB).

Some would argue that they must call sin by its name. That is surely true, but harsh denunciation that attempts to do the work of the Holy Spirit oversteps the directives of the "ministry of reconciliation." The Apostle Paul wrote, "When someone becomes a Christian he becomes a brand new person inside. He is not the same any more. A new life has begun! All these new things are from God who brought us back to Himself through what Christ Jesus did. And God has given us the privilege of urging everyone to come into His favor and be reconciled to Him. For God was in Christ, restoring the world to Himself, no longer counting men's sins against them but blotting them out. This is the wonderful message He has given us to tell others. We are Christ's ambassadors. God is using us to speak to you: we beg you, as though Christ Himself were here pleading with you, receive the love He offers you—be reconciled to God" (2 Cor. 5:17-20, LB). Our task is to woo people into the kingdom, not to keep them out.

Guilt-Ridden Christians

I meet other Christians who face the problem of guilt. There's a certain kind of preaching which cripples personalities, forcing people to feel degraded and rejected so that even the blood of Christ does not bring them peace of heart. These people are saved from the guilt of sin and are heavenbound, but they are so bruised psychologically and emotionally they cannot enjoy their Christian lives. We need to understand that there is no sin too big for God.

In Galatians 3:1-3, we read of Christians who forgot that only the free grace of God produces perfection. To the Corinthians Paul spoke of a "worldly sorrow which brings death"

(2 Cor. 7:8-11, NIV). In modern English we would call it remorse, the process of blaming and punishing oneself for sin and wrongdoing. Remorse is deadly if it does not turn one to Christ for relief. The same passage speaks of "godly sorrow that brings life." This is repentance that spurs confession and allows us to leave our burden of sin at the Cross. Trying to carry past sins by ourselves will crush us.

There is a story told of a man riding down a country road on a donkey. He has a 200-pound sack of wheat on his shoulders. A passerby suggested: "Why don't you take the sack off your shoulders and put it on the saddle?" and the rider retorted, "You don't think I'd ask the donkey to carry all that weight, do you?" Many Christians who have been freed by Christ from the weight of their sins have been bent again by someone's legalism and false purity. Christ frees us of both our sins and our guilt when we know He forgives and forgets!

Complete Reconciliation

The heartening assurance which comes from Bill and Becky and from the poignant story of Jesus meeting the woman caught in adultery is that Christ's forgiveness releases us from the past. We must appropriate this forgiveness and give this forgiveness without reservation to our brothers and sisters in Christ. In his book *Screwtape Letters* (Macmillan), C. S. Lewis spoke of this when he wrote, "If I, knowing what I am, can call myself a Christian, why can't he, being what he seems to be, call himself the same name?" This kind of righteousness truly exceeds the "righteousness of the scribes and Pharisees" (see Matt. 5:20).

The oneness and healing demonstrated in Bill and Becky's experience is happily repeated by thousands of others. One of the unique truths of the Christian message is that people can know complete reconciliation to God, to themselves, and to one another. It can, however, be only theological truth for pastors' sermons unless we activate this truth in our personal lives and our personal relationships.

The open-faced, exuberant testimony of Bill and the hesitant yet confident growth of Becky, with the new life and secure radiance of little Ann, are to me reminders of the truly marvelous nature of the "unspeakable gift of grace that is ours in Christ" (see 2 Cor. 9:14-15).

Study Questions

Read 2 Corinthians 7:8-11; 5:17-21; 1 Corinthians 6:9-11; Matthew 5:30-32; 23; John 8:1-11; Matthew 5:20, 28; Ephesians 2:8-9; Galatians 3:1-7.

1. What righteousness was lacking in the scribes and Pharisees?
2. How is grace needed in the lives of Christians?
3. What obstacles would a person like Becky face in your church?
4. Are men less guilty than women in cases of sexual promiscuity? Why or why not?
5. Imagine what problems Bill might face with his family back home and suggest how he may overcome them.

11

Who Made Tammy Die?

When we read of tragedies in other people's lives we shake our heads and say, "Isn't that terrible?" Sometimes our concern lasts into our table prayers or family conversation. The cares of our own lives, however, usually keep us from personal involvement. When tragedy hits those close to us, we are seldom prepared.

I was in the middle of a volleyball game at youth camp when a voice blared over the loudspeaker, "Telephone for Jay Kesler." "Oh, no," I thought, "why can't they let me finish a game?" I was sure it was some administrative "crisis" which could wait until I returned home.

I left my team of teenagers and grudgingly walked to a phone a block away. Over the years I've learned to pray before each phone conversation. If someone on the other end needs something I have, I want God's wisdom to help them in the best way I can. Perfunctorily I breathed my prayer and said, "Hello." I was surprised to hear the voice of my wife, Janie.

"Jay," she said anxiously, "we need you at home right now. Something awful has happened."

Concerned about my father's heart condition, I asked if it was he. "No," Janie answered slowly, "it's Tammy. She's dead."

She then told me how my brother-in-law, Ray, one of my closest friends in high school, had accidentally driven over his five-year-old daughter with his milk truck. It was one of those tragedies which make you say, "It can't be! It's too awful!"

Since Ray began his day at 3:00 A.M., he frequently came home in the middle of his work day to share breakfast with his family. Often one of the children would ask to go with him to help finish his milk delivery route.

On this midsummer morning it was Tammy who went along. Daddy and daughter—who could be happier? Ray put the truck in reverse and carefully backed out of the driveway as he had many times before, and then Tammy changed her mind and jumped out of the truck just as he shifted into first gear to start forward. She was run over by the rear wheels, managed to get up, ran a few steps to the house crying, "Mommy, Mommy, help me, help me," then collapsed in the front yard. She later died in surgery.

Janie's words numbed me. *What can I do? How is Ray doing? How's Jackie? Who is comforting the other children? God, why do these things happen?* These and a hundred other thoughts raced through my mind. At that moment I dreaded being God's representative. How could I get to Ray and Jackie? Was there some way to explain my feelings to the kids playing volleyball? I couldn't expect them to fully understand. Dare they know how my own faith was being tested, that at this moment I resented God? I said good-bye to Janie and promised I'd be there as fast as I could make travel arrangements. I opted to share the news with the youth leaders and kids and asked for their prayers which I knew would be of value when I arrived at Jackie and Ray's house.

During the three-hour drive alone, I wondered why college and seminary hadn't given a course on what to say at times like this. "O God," I prayed, "suppose it were one of my children? O Christ, please be with Ray and Jackie. Especially Ray. Please, Lord, give me something to say. Help me to do the right thing. Maybe it's all a terrible nightmare. Perhaps Tammy is better off this way than crippled for life. No, I know some wonderful, useful, fulfilled people who are crippled. God, why does this have to be?"

I remembered a prayer I had prayed as a teenager when I wrecked my dad's car. Standing by the car with the front fender gone and both doors caved in, I closed my eyes and thought of mustard seeds and prayed, "God, I pray it didn't happen!" Slowly I opened my eyes only to realize the foolishness of such a prayer. Life is real; facts are facts. A Christian's car acts just like a non-Christian's car in a highway skid.

I arrived at Jackie and Ray's home and went into the house through the kitchen as rural Indiana people do with close friends and family. Janie was trying to get everyone to sit down and eat something. "You need it," she said.

We all search for ways to say something useful when we feel useless. What we would like to do if we could, is to bring back a loved one to life again. Jesus did it twice, why not again? "Greater things than these shall [you] do; because I go to the Father" (John 14:12, NASB).

Jackie saw me and ran into my arms. We hugged each other and I wondered why it took tragedy for a brother to hug his sister. I held her and listened to her anguish. "Oh, Jay, it's awful. It hurts so bad. I almost wish we never had Tammy."

I didn't know what to say. I responded with something like, "Oh, Jackie, you don't mean that . . . I'm so sorry."

I was sorry. Sorry for Tammy, sorry for Jackie, sorry for the other kids, sorry for Janie, sorry for grandmas and grandpas, but also sorry that my God had created a world that often goes sour, and in which answers and rationalizations seem ludicrous beside a dead five-year-old child.

I began to question why God let these things happen. And if He couldn't stop them why didn't He do a miracle afterwards? "O God," I prayed, "it would be so simple for you to bring just one small child back to life." Yet I knew, except for those in the Gospels, many people have asked for the same thing and been disappointed.

I began to feel guilty thinking these thoughts. *Why am I embarrassed?* I asked myself. *I love Him; I trust Him. I still believe He does all things well. I don't believe His ear is heavy or His arm shortened. This is just beyond my grasp now. I know Romans 11:33 says "His ways [are] past finding out," but why doesn't He explain it? Why are people who never have doubts considered so strong? Why am I expected to come up with pat answers? Why can't I show grief? Jesus did.*

The thoughts tumbled around in my head while I took my place at the table and said simply, "I'm sorry, Ray. Yes, thanks, I'll have another cup of coffee."

After a long interval, as if no gap had occurred since we met in the kitchen, Jackie said, "But that's the way love is, isn't it? If you love, you're going to hurt, aren't you?"

I responded, thankful for another glimpse of truth. "Yes, Jackie, I think you're right. If you love there's the chance to get hurt. The only way to insure we'll never hurt is not to be involved, never get close, insulate ourselves from care for others."

I could describe the marvelous way that God worked in this family situation, but my point is that Christians must experience sorrow, and sorrow may try our faith. Non-Christians can write off life's trials as unfortunate twists of fate, bad breaks at best, so they "live and let live" or "eat, drink, and be merry for tomorrow we die."

For the Christian it is quite another thing. Is God the author of evil? Is He causally connected to all our experiences? Does He jam one car into another on the freeway? Do we limit God's sovereignty by saying man has freedom? Does God say, "I think I'll give this child leukemia and this one a pony"? Can He do things in a holy way which would make me evil if I did them? Is bad "good" or somehow justified when God does it?

My purpose is not to attempt a complete answer to the problem of evil, but to suggest some help in the context of this traumatic experience.

The Evil Intruder

First, when God completed the Creation, He said it was "very good" (Gen. 1:31). This good included the creation of man made in His image. Then evil entered after the Creation was complete. God did not create a bad and good tree—the tree had the capacity for good or bad in man's use of it. Evil is an intruder in God's creation that was welcomed by man's choice. God could have spared man this freedom to choose and made him like plants, animals, and inanimate objects that carry out their programmed functions. But then we couldn't have known love, only loyalty. "If you love, separation is going to hurt."

In a world of order, rain does fall on the just and the unjust. Two objects cannot occupy the same space at the same time, so car wrecks kill Christians and non-Christians. Suffering is part of the scene if man is to move from sin-flawed creation back to perfect harmony with God.

The Christian has a unique ministry to those who see the world as happenstance, a cosmic accident. The Christian affirms in his suffering that the "human project" is worthwhile —it's better to have "loved and lost than never to have loved at all." In order to experience love and enjoy meaningful relationships we must take risks. These risks sometimes bring tragedy—which also can bring God near. Without man's capacity for evil and failure, he could not know the wonder of holiness and victory. That knowledge remains hidden to people estranged from God.

God's Unchangeable Laws

It sounds reassuring to say that there are no accidents for the Christian. If this means that God instead of human error causes all calamities, the statement is false. If, on the other hand, "accident" means that there is never any circumstance beyond God's power to transform into blessing, then truly there are no accidents. But to say glibly that there are no accidents is to suggest that God causes all heartache, pain, and sorrow. To say bad things are good things is to play games with words and to trifle with God's own Word.

There is an awesome risk inhabiting our imperfect world. Human sin unleashed the destructive forces of disease and death and discordant elements. God mercifully restrains these forces, but he does not usually suspend the natural laws by which they operate. A disastrous earthquake tells us something is seriously wrong in our universe—something that can be righted when we return to harmony with our Creator.

Good is Greater Than Evil

Our most heartening realization comes from the news that

God did not exempt Himself from the evil consequences of His crippled creation. God in Jesus Christ became "a man of sorrows, and acquainted with grief" (Isa. 53:3). He did not use supernatural means to escape the nature of creation. Jesus experienced hunger, fatigue, the death of friends, personal rejection and torture at the hands of cruel men.

Bad is bad; evil is evil; good is good. But Christ showed us how our reactions can turn evil to good, pain to profit, sorrow to comfort. In this sense the promise in Romans 8:28 is realizable. "All things work together for good," when we indeed "love God [and are] . . . the called according to His purpose." God is greater than evil; He will eventually right all wrongs, but even now He is the avowed enemy, not the promoter, of evil and death.

The Christian, therefore, has his confidence in God though he has not resolved all the mind-bending problems and incongruities of life. Faith is not a matter of covering error and evil with Band-Aids of pious phrases. Faith is knowing God cares in the midst of calamity, that He gives solace in the center of a storm. Christian victory neither denies evil nor forgets God.

Christianity is Not a Reality Cop-out

The Christian faith is the only adequate way to deal with the totality of experience in this life and the life to come.

When we accept life with its pains, joys, and perplexities, we realize our profound need of Jesus Christ in whom "is all the fulness of the Godhead bodily, and we are complete in Him who is the head of all principality and power" (Col. 2:9-10).

I will never forget a conversation with a young man at Chicago's LaSalle Street Church one Sunday evening. The area lies, depending on the time of day, in the shadow of

Carl Sandburg Village or Cabrini Green. One is an exclusive, high-rise apartment complex for upper middle-class professionals; the other is a high-rise, low income, high crime, black ghetto. The congregation is a cross section of the community and a result of the neighborhood experiences.

This young man jumped down my throat with both feet. He told me of the tragic lives in the community, the inequities, and the heartaches. He told me that as a result of what he had seen he didn't believe in God. I asked him, "Tell me what God you don't believe in; maybe I don't believe in Him either." Sure enough, the god he thought was the God of the Bible was not. He presented a god that was so inadequate and petty, so full of triviality, capriciousness, and vengeance that I could never accept him. In fact, if I knew a human being like that he would be locked up.

Our God is not smaller than our ideals. He is infinitely greater than the finest man we can imagine. Our trouble is that we do not know God as He is. But He is revealed to us in Jesus Christ, and our imperfect understanding can be reassured by His perfect love. God didn't kill Tammy, but He can resurrect hope and joy in all who mourn because of their Tammys.

Study Questions

Read Romans 8:28-29; 11:33; Job 2:10; James 1:12-17; 4:1-2; Genesis 1:31; John 16:20-23, 33; 17:15; 1 Peter 5:6-11; Matthew 5:43-48; 2 Corinthians 1:3-4; 4:11; Philippians 2:5-11.

1. What evils would not exist on the earth if man did not have a will?
2. How do we protect ourselves from the risks of living? Can we really experience love if we evade its hazards?
3. Do you have any deep wounds covered by a band-aid of

thin words? How do you handle the pain "in the mean-time"?

4. Among the unchurched people you know, are there any who seem to have decided to "curse God and die"? How might they be helped?

5. When a Christian cries at a funeral, is this a poor testimony to unbelievers—or something else?

6. What relationship do you see between 2 Corinthians 1:24 and Philippians 2:5-11?

7. If the counsel in this chapter leaves gaps in your faith, where might you find additional help?

12

No Chip Off the Old Block

Like most parents, Larry and Hazel loved their children and willingly sacrificed for their education and welfare. But when they spoke to me, they were heartbroken. Their two oldest daughters had attended Christian liberal arts colleges and done well. One daughter married a young business executive during her senior year and still managed to graduate with her class. Their second daughter had shown a "lot of common sense" in breaking off an aimless relationship. "She doesn't seem to be in a hurry to settle down," said Hazel, "and that's OK with us."

"All in all, we're pretty relaxed about the girls," Larry continued, "but our son Roger is giving us fits. You name it and he's been into it. It's as if he's determined to be on the wrong side of everything."

"He's not really a bad boy," said Hazel. "He's smart in his own way, but we don't understand him. At first we thought he was going through a stage. You know how every kid has to disagree with his parents' values. But he's been out of high school for a year and doesn't want to do anything with his life. He talks about going to Oregon and living in a cabin in the woods near a hippie colony."

As Larry and Hazel poured out their disappointments, I discovered Roger had never been interested in studying. In high school he read, but mostly noncredit material. "Roger was always reading science fiction or novels which were too embarrassing for us to read," said Hazel. "We're not prudes, and I tried to have an open mind about it, but then he started to neglect personal hygiene and clothes like we couldn't afford to buy at the Salvation Army.

"Can you imagine wearing the same pair of jeans for a month and an old army jacket that never did fit? It's almost as if he has a list of things we like and has set himself against them.

"He doesn't misbehave in a specific way; he's not in trouble with the law, and he's respectful, better than a lot of kids his age. He feels the draft dodgers were right, the school system is a waste of time, and he's convinced that to go into our business is some sort of compromise. Can you imagine a paint and wallpaper store being immoral?

"He wouldn't think of voting in an election, and thinks we're silly to watch the news. Yet he will play with children in the vacant lot and sit for hours looking at the birds and squirrels in the park. He will defend homosexuals and their cause, yet isn't one of them. He defends blacks but says they're foolish for trying to make it in the system. He says they're in for a big disappointment if they get what they're after, but doesn't think they will.

"Can you imagine a boy, raised in our home with sisters who've turned out all right, becoming a Henry David Thoreau of the '70s? I guess it could be worse, but we had dreams of him being successful and now we don't know what to do.

Don't tell us to pray, because we've prayed and prayed, and he only gets more determined than ever. We're not ignorant, intolerant people, but we're worried he'll end up just wasting his life."

Ten years ago this pattern was common in many families, but now things have changed. Youth are following more conventional paths and generally the "problems of youth" are easier for parents to deal with, probably because they are more like the problems of the '50s. Alcohol is "in" again, going steady is back in vogue, and sports are gaining popularity. The youth of the mid-'70s are seeking technical education and are interested to a larger degree in "getting ahead." Even the idea of a conventional home seems to be more attractive since the movie *Love Story*. But this is little comfort for a family with a son like Roger.

Today most suburban middle-class youths have rejected his life-style. Is Roger the last of a disappearing breed? Is he some sort of anachronism? Or has his value structure found a permanent place in American culture? Time will tell whether it's permanent or not, but many youth have been affected by the central themes of Roger's viewpoint. The questions and difficulties behind Roger's disillusionment with society are basic questions for all. We might disagree with Roger's response and criticize his "dropping out," but as Christians we need to examine these questions and come to some satisfactory personal answers.

Experience Versus Facts

Our society says that all people should go to school, including college, follow the prescribed curriculum, get good grades and prepare for useful and gainful employment. Roger has a two-pronged argument against this.

"First," he says, "schools once were aimed at preparing

people to cope with human affairs and showed people how to appreciate the richness of their world. But much of what is taught today is irrelevant to life. The meaningful lessons of life are not in "flatland"—facts, figures, skills—but are also sensuous—experienced and felt. Schools prepare you to be more and more narrow, to specialize. I'd rather make a pair of moccasins with my own hands and experience how it happened than buy the best pair of shoes going."

Human Values Versus Things

His second argument charges that today's education sees people as cogs in some gear of modern technological machinery. "They (Roger's term for the establishment) used to give you a one-button education when machines had one button, then a two-button education when machines had two. Now that they have three or four buttons, they teach each of us to specialize on our button. People exist for the system, not the other way around. It's all backwards. I'm interested in human values, not things."

John, the Unconventional

As we think of Larry and Hazel and their son's unorthodox life-style, try to imagine the feelings of Zacharias and Elizabeth (Luke 1:11-15) as their son John adopted an unconventional method of serving God. There was a rabbinical school, an accepted path for a young man who wanted to enter the priesthood and become a rabbi. For John, the accepted curriculum and the garb of the traditional clergy seemed to be irrelevant (Matthew 3). Is it possible that the message of the Rogers in the '70s contains prophetic implications for all of us too?

John didn't have a problem to be cured; he had a message to deliver. It was a minority message which needed to be heard by his contemporaries. It seems worthwhile to examine any parallel before we rejoice at the passing of Roger's breed from our midst.

Jesus, the Radical
It is also evident to all who study the life of Christ that the religious system espoused by the Pharisees had distorted God's intent for man. The Law was the all-important issue, and man was its slave. Jesus aroused great opposition when He challenged this distortion (Matt. 12:1-14). The Sabbath and the law were not as important to Jesus as were the people (Matt. 5:17-48). The institutions were incorrectly related to man, and Jesus had to challenge them (Mark 2:27).

Misplaced Priorities
There is a message in this for modern man and his institutions. We certainly reject the idea of destroying institutions as advocated by revolutionists; the technology and institutions are not necessarily bad, but if they are misplaced in our priorities, then Roger and other young critics have a point.

But it's still hard for Zacharias and Elizabeth, Joseph and Mary, and Larry and Hazel. I don't say the parallels are exact or even correct, but I am saying that they beg investigation and careful analysis by Christians who want to live wisely for their Lord.

Sensitivity to Right and Wrong
Roger's third challenge regards war. He felt that his friends were justified and noble when they refused to participate in a conflict they felt was evil.

Roger's problem is not with war as such, but with the issue of individual conscience and obedience to the State. This issue was adjudicated for Germans at Nuremberg after World War I.

The victorious Allies decreed that functionaries who followed orders repugnant to humane moral standards should be punished as war criminals. Roger adopts this logic and feels people should obey their conscience regardless of what the government says.

Man's conscience should never be subservient to the State, though his body is never entirely his own. I did not have to wait until my son was of draft age to be met with this dilemma. He was about five when he and his two sisters listened to me read the Christmas story from the Bible. I should have been on guard because the year before he had said the wise men should have brought candy to Jesus rather than gold, frankincense, and myrrh because "He probably would have liked it better."

This time he asked why the soldiers killed the babies in Bethlehem. I explained the king wanted to be sure Jesus didn't become king, so he killed all the boys of Jesus' age. "Was the king bigger than the soldiers?" he asked.

"No," I said, "he was about regular size."

"Was there more than one king?"

"No, just one."

"Did the soldiers have babies of their own at home?"

"Yes, I suppose so."

"Didn't they feel bad killing babies?"

"Yes, I'm sure they did." (It's embarrassing to get trapped by a five year old!)

"Didn't they know it was wrong to kill babies?"

"Yes, I think so, but that's the way it is with kings and soldiers. The soldiers have to do what the king says. That's just the way it is."

"I'm sorry, Daddy," he pleaded, as if it had just happened this week. "If they knew it was wrong, they shouldn't have done it even if the king said so!"

I was frustrated to be detoured from the manger story and was conscious he had touched a protected nerve in my life. While I had felt that defining "swaddling clothes" was important, he brought me back. For many years I've struggled to keep alive a sensitivity to right and wrong even though "all the kids are doing it."

Christians have struggled with "situation ethics" for centuries. The "divine right of kings" was well established at the time of the American revolution. Even John Wesley preached against the colonies because of the Scripture advocating loyalty to the sovereign. He could not see King George as more evil than the Caesar that Peter spoke of in his epistle (1 Peter 2:13-18). Yet there are repeated examples of individual conscience defying authority in the Old and New Testaments. The exiled Hebrew trio were thrown in a fiery furnace, Daniel was thrown to lions, and John the Baptist lost his head for challenging monarchs. The Old Testament prophets constantly faced death by a political power on the basis of divine right.

Our sons and daughters will need our careful and prayer-filled counsel as they try to resolve difficult issues. Most generations have had their share of sophomoric youths who have rejected the structure and life-style of their parents. Perhaps we shouldn't be so anxious to knock the stars out of their eyes as they seek a "higher way." In most cases the practical accommodations of survival will do it soon enough. Also, the abrasiveness of living in a tentative position will polarize most. It is unfortunate when adults allow themselves to get like concrete—"all mixed up and permanently set." Let's face it, most of us spend most of our time reinforcing our prejudices by what we read and our choice of friends. Prejudices based on casual preference rather than sound information should be questioned with low heat and high respect by both generations.

Man's Purpose

Whether Roger will "waste his life" is open for debate. In the light of eternity, how many of man's accomplishments are worthwhile and ultimate? In light of Scripture, it is clear that what man is outweighs his functions. Solomon spent many hours contemplating man's accomplishments and existence and concluded all was vanity. It is evident from the Bible that man is not simply a means to an end. Man was created to share God's glory by glorifying Him (Matt. 5:16; 2 Cor. 9:13). Peter explained on the day of Pentecost that the launching of the Gospel marked an end to some cherished traditions of men: "Your sons and daughters shall prophesy, and your young men shall see visions" (Acts 2:17).

There are few easy solutions to the problems facing modern youth, but beneath their hair, clothing, irreverence, despair, and sometimes anger or indifference are some seeds of spiritual creativity.

Not so incidentally—Roger has applied for short-term missionary service in Africa. What do they say? "All's well that ends well!"

Study Questions

Read Luke 1:11-25; Matthew 3; 5:17-48; 12:1-14; 22:15-21; Mark 2:27; 1 Peter 2:13-18; Daniel 3:13-19; 6:10-15; Jeremiah 32:1-3; 37:15; 38:2-6; Ecclesiastes 3:9-12.

1. What parallels do you see between John the Baptist's life-style and that of some dissenting youth we might meet on campus today?
2. What rank does the Bible give to man in God's creation? And what rank does the social climate of our society give him?
3. Are there areas of church life where human values are subordinated to things?

4. What are some things that belong to Caesar and what is God's? (Matt. 22:15-21)
5. How do you think Jesus would answer the question: What is success?

13

No "Justas" Around Here

"Jay, I no longer believe I can accomplish God's will as a high school teacher," said a good friend one day.

I had admired Bob for a long time. Like many of my teacher friends, he was highly motivated and viewed teaching as a job with a ministry to people. To see his disillusionment now hurt me.

I've watched other teachers and administrators become cynical about the system, student apathy, and lack of motivation in co-workers, and Bob's defeated look was a blow to me. I found myself thinking, *Can't anyone make it on the firing line? Why does everyone who works with people seem to give up and retreat to more predictable things?*

This was an exaggeration, of course, but it seems that so many give up while the "drones" stay and draw their pay. I have also been discouraged to see so many laymen leave secular occupations to enter "full-time Christian service," as if they couldn't serve the Lord among the people who need Him so much. I asked Bob what he planned to do.

"I don't know," he said, "but I'm defeated. Our principal is just coasting. He doesn't want to make waves and is waiting for retirement. My fellow teachers lack motivation and I feel like I'm banging my head against a brick wall. I'm not going to quit, but I need your prayers."

After honestly sharing his feelings, Bob seemed less tense but I could tell he was expecting some answer. I prayed for a breakthrough to help not only him but the many laymen who feel small in the midst of the system.

Once I saw a film about John Henry, the "steel-driving man," who was pitted against a steam drill. With bulging muscles and sweat flowing from a determined brow, John Henry drove and slammed away with his sledge hammer. But the inevitable happened. The steam drill outlasted him and he collapsed to the pound-pound of the steam drill in his ears. "Lord," I prayed, "please come to Bob's rescue. Don't let the system crush him. Show us something which will give hope for his sake and the sake of the kids in the school who so desperately need Christian models."

A few days later Bob said, "Hey, brother, good news. I've found another teacher who knows the Lord and we've decided to start praying for our school."

Good, I thought. *Now we've doubled our strength and the burden seems lighter.*

Within a few weeks eight teachers were studying the Bible and praying each morning before school. "You can just feel the difference," said Bob. "We're praying and encouraging each other and things are starting to move. We've asked the Lord for a bunch of young guys we can take to the Fellowship of Christian Athletes camp this summer and the coach is excited about it!"

The principal retired that summer and a competent educator took his place. The prayer meetings continued along with the formation of a Fellowship of Christian Athletes chapter, Campus Life club, and several church youth groups. In addition, several teachers with their wives and families found Christ.

I'm sure Bob would be the last person to take credit for being the central person in this awakening, yet it's a fact that things happened when one desperate man turned to God and allowed His power to work through him.

No "Justas" in the Body

I wish I had a dollar for every layman and woman who has said to me, "I'm *just* a teacher." "I'm *just* a plumber." "I'm *just* a housewife." "I'm *just* a computer programmer." "I'm *just* a secretary." "I'm *just* a lawyer . . ." According to Scripture, there is no such thing as a "justa." It is contrary to New Testament reality. The concept of the Early Church was a body made up of many parts, none of which is more important than the other (Rom. 12:3-5).

This body is a unity and each part needs the other (Eph. 4:16). We are one in Christ. In Him we are complete, full and whole (Col. 2:9-10). This wholeness speaks of the completeness of our salvation. Nothing more can be added except the appropriation of riches we have been promised.

We Need Each Other

Though we are completely acceptable to God in Christ, we are not whole in our character and conduct. All of us are flat-sided and need the help of other body members to fill out our deficiencies. It is impossible for the pastor alone to accomplish this.

A pastor can help his congregation become more complete in areas of biblical knowledge and application. Laymen in turn can help him overcome the restricted clergical point of view. Some members of the body are secure, others are intimidated. Some can profit by criticism, some are defensive. Others are outgoing, while some are protective. The body of Christ is formed by Him to supplement the strengths and counter the weaknesses of its members because none of us are complete in ourselves.

A friend of mine put it this way: "It's like the 45 r.p.m. records the kids buy: one side is good and the other is lousy. When we in the church glue our bad sides together we can play a pretty good tune." Not a bad illustration of the body, or of marriage too!

Unconditional Love

Safe in Christ's love, we can remove our masks because fear is conquered. We are sure the love of the brotherhood will never allow us to be "drummed out of the corps." In the same way that Christ's love is unaffected by our performance, we accept one another on the basis of intrinsic value rather than conformity to ourselves.

Such unity gives us strength, and when we fail we are shored up by the strength of others. We bear one another's burdens, and they become lighter. In this unity we are no longer compelled to make others in our image. The cookie cutter with which we attempt to duplicate ourselves in others is discarded and we allow the Holy Spirit to shape their lives. Since we appreciate the long-suffering and patience of God toward us, we allow others time to grow in grace and knowledge of the Lord Jesus. We are heartened to know the unity of the body of Christ is not only local but global. In fact, it spans time and unites us with those saints who have gone on before and those who shall follow (John 17:20-21).

Look at a typical congregation: each person has different facial features, variety in body structure, and distinctive tastes in clothing. As this diversity is the spice of life, it is the potential for dynamic ministry when dedicated to God.

A single method or emphasis would not accomplish God's purposes. It would hit a few targets and miss the rest. The only set strategy in the New Testament is the divine-human strategy: the variety of human experiences meeting the vast resources of God. Successful Christians need each other!

Individual Dignity
There is also individual dignity in this body. No one is less deserving of care and honor than the other (1 Cor. 12:25-27). Those who serve behind the scenes and those who have less pleasant tasks are as worthy as those who are prominent and brilliant.

I once visited a plumber friend on a construction site. We watched while the pipes he had installed were covered with several inches of concrete. As the concrete flowed he said, "It dosn't matter if anyone ever sees those fittings again; I've done my work with excellence and to the glory of God." Every act of life has meaning to the Christian and is important for the full functioning of the body of believers (Col. 3:17).

More Christians should read *The Practice of the Presence of God*. This writing by a medieval monk named Brother Lawrence reveals how a Christian who envisioned himself in some important public ministry celebrated his service to God as a cook working over pots and pans and potatoes. God could perform functions without people, but He chose to accomplish in fellowship and partnership with His people.

It is a gross misunderstanding of God's strategy to think the ideal Christian is one who is in "full-time service." It is a victory for Satan which separates clergy and laity into performers and spectators, and makes Sunday within the church walls the sufficient service of God. The Church of Jesus must gather for worship and learning, but it must also function daily in classrooms, laundromats, factories, trains, planes, trucks, at the drafting boards, down in construction excavations, over coffee, under shade trees, and on playing fields. The Body of Christ functions wherever believers are trying to serve Him and one another.

Unique Gifts

It is dishonoring to your Creator to think of yourself as a "justa." Scripture teaches that each member of the body has been given a unique gift which equips him for the function to which he has been called. Some Christians have more than one gift, but each gift came from the same Source—the Holy Spirit. Each person's gift may be manifested in a different way than his neighbor's, but each is given for the body's common good (1 Cor. 12:1-11).

Every Christian should discover and exercise his spiritual gifts (12:31). The hierarchy of spiritual gifts is put into perspective for us in the 13th and 14th chapters of 1 Corinthians. Throughout church history, there has been a great deal of division over the use of glossolalia, or speaking in tongues. Some have attached spiritual pride to this experience and insisted it be an experience for the entire body. Some great saints have had this experience and many have not. It is a shame to miss what Paul called the greater gifts while arguing about a lesser one.

The Apostle Paul gave the Romans some practical illustrations of some of the body gifts (Rom. 12:6-13). God can use any and all of our gifts for His glory and in every walk of life. As we read the New Testament, we discover the church began as a lay movement. There were few full-time Christian workers. Many were educated in the hard schools of experience and were salted throughout every layer of society. They penetrated the Roman army and brought Christ's flavor into Caesar's household.

There is a theology that makes God big by making man small. Man is indeed weak when struggling in his own strength, but the Architect of the universe has created us in His image to accomplish amazing things through our redeemed and dedicated personalities.

God's multifaceted strategy works as we allow Him to use us right where we are. There is no such thing as a "justa," for God will work in all His people to do His good pleasure (Phil. 2:13).

Study Questions

Read Romans 12:1-21; 1 Corinthians 12—14; Ephesians 4:4-16.
1. How does the "eyes and ears" or "hands and feet" illustration apply to your church today?
2. How effectively is the body principle working in your church?
3. Is there an implication in Christendom that the really dedicated Christians are "full time"? Discuss.
4. Is unity achieved effectively by organization and planning, or something else?
5. Do you know what your gifts are or your place in the body? Would your friends agree?